CHANGING ORGANIZATIONAL CULTURE

A Study of the National Government

Philip M. Nufrio

University Press of America,® Inc.
Lanham · New York · Oxford

Copyright © 2001 by
University Press of America,® Inc.
4720 Boston Way
Lanham, Maryland 20706

12 Hid's Copse Rd.
Cumnor Hill, Oxford OX2 9JJ

Library of Congress Cataloging-in-Publication Data

Nufrio, Philip M.
Changing organizational culture :
a study of the national government / Philip M. Nufrio.
p.   cm
Includes bibliographical references and index.
1. Corporate culture. 2. Corporate culture—United States.
3. Organizational change. I. Title.
HM791 .N84 2001   352.3'67'0973—dc21   2001035296 CIP

ISBN 0-7618-2020-5 (pbk. : alk. paper)

DEDICATED TO
My mother Lenore Nufrio and my son Philip Michael

Contents

Preface

The need for research of this kind was impressed on me more than 20 years ago when I was a Management Analyst in the Executive Office of the President. I was one of many management consultants employed, on loan from the federal cabinet agencies, to the Executive Office of the President within the President's Reorganization Project. During this experience I remember how many of my colleagues in the field of Organization Development struggled with the challenge of how do you change the culture a large government agency. My work on the President's Reorganization Project left me with two impressions: (1) It triggered both my interest and continuing frustration in understanding the nature of organizational culture change in government; (2) It demonstrated to me the need for better knowledge in both the planning, implementation and evaluation of organizational change efforts like the President's Reorganization Project.

In 1995 when I was a Ph.D. candidate in the Public Administration at Rutgers University, it struck me that the issues that I experienced within the President's Reorganization Project did not dissipate when both the Reagan and Clinton administrations continued an almost century-old attempt to reform the federal cabinet agencies. It was clear that the reform information available to government executives and managers, albeit impressionistic, remained anecdotal and sketchy, and was hardly measurable. The issue before the field of public administration still remains: how can successful change be both planned and evaluated for its impact.

This study represents a beginning attempt to provide a sound and systematically measurable model needed by government executives, managers and social scientists interested in both the execution and evaluation of administrative reform. To provide a more systematic *Changing Organizational Culture: A Study of the National Government* and measurable model, I had used some of the well-established univariate and multivariate statistics employed in the social science field. However I applied them in a way never addressed in the literature. This book illustrates how these tools could be employed to assess the nature of organizational culture change over time.

My research encompasses 21 federal cabinet agencies, and attitude work force survey data collected by the U.S. Merit Systems Protection Board in 1992 and 1996. After this book is circulated, many readers will undoubtedly take issue with my goals and research methodology. I welcome these reactions so that maybe we can improve the knowledge of government reform as it enters a new era and century of practice.

To analyze the massive amount of survey data (more than 10,000 observations) collected on the 21 federal cabinet agencies required many viii

months of comparing agency to agency in order to discover patterns and draw comparisons on the dimensions of organizational culture.

I must thank my friend and mentor, Dr. Raphael Caprio, who pushed me to my limit so that I could answer the important question of organizational culture change. I must also thank Mr. David Orden of Rutgers University whose knowledge and assistance in working with massive data sets accomplished the Herculean feat of collapsing two major time sets of data that were compared.

My research effort can be understood, in large part, as an attempt to track and evaluate important dimensions of organizational culture from 1992 through 1996. This occurred during the important years in which the Clinton Administration attempted to reform the culture of the federal cabinet agencies. It is my hope that my research and insights will help both government executives and scholars in resolving the many dilemmas with which administrative reform must cope with now and in the future.

There are many others I wish to acknowledge in research of this scope. Raphael Caprio, Pauline Frederick Hicks, James Garnett, Hindy Schachter, Gerald Miller, Marcia Whicker, Marc Holzer, Jade Berry, Joseph Santora and my mother Lenore who pored over my earlier manuscript. They both nurtured and coaxed the education of this author in this work. The late Dr. Marcia Whicker deserves special mention for her conscientious and constructive suggestions to my thinking. My thanks also go to Dr. John Crumb of the U.S. Merit Systems Protection for providing the secondary data used in this study. The National Performance Review project in the Office of Vice President Al Gore provided substantial cooperation in giving me access to federal executives I interviewed in the field segment of this study.

The Graduate School of Public Administration at Rutgers University-Newark provided much logistical and moral support for my research. Ms. Marilyn Johnson did a skillful, meticulous job of typing the manuscript.

A special appreciation goes to my mother Lenore, my late father Felix, my son Philip, my life long friend Dr. Frank Polverino. Their love and support made the completion of this research possible. Finally I wish to thank Kaicho Tadashi Nakumura, Shihan William Best, and Kioshi Nan Baldwin for their leadership and inspiration in following the "sincere path" of Seido Juke.

Chapter 1

Changing Organizational Culture: A Study of the National Government

The Research Problem

In the early 1980s with American corporations losing their competitive edge in the world economy, the term "organization culture" emerged as the new management catch phrase. The organization culture literature addressed various aspects of organizational life including leadership, hierarchy, productivity, conflict, and power.

Organizational culture is seen in terms of the informal, normative dimensions of organizational life. (Blau, 1955; Peters and Waterman, 1982; Kanter, 1984; Ouchi, 1985; Schein, 1985, 1991; March and Olsen, 1989; Martin, 1993; Argyris, 1993; and Bennis 1993). As interpreted in this research organizational culture signifies the beliefs undergirding an organization's behavior (Kanter, 1984; Ouchi, 1985; Schein, 1985, 1991; and, March and Olsen, 1989). An organization's culture develops as it absorbs various internal and external stimuli, such as leadership patterns, political pressures, the organization's goals, and its structural mechanisms.

Around the nation and across institutions, leaders and researchers jumped on the "culture bandwagon" as they attempted to improve organizational productivity and effectiveness via some explanation of the organization's culture (e.g. values, rituals, ceremonies and leadership patterns). In 1992, Bill Clinton jumped on this bandwagon when he created the National Performance Review (NPR) project under the direction of Vice President Al Gore. The NPR is both programmatic and process-oriented, seeking to change the culture of the federal government and the cabinet executive agencies.

NPR was implemented in two phases (NPR I and NPR II). NPR's goals and operating strategies (Gore, 1993) sought to "reinvigorate the entire national government" by moving federal programs and bureaucracies from a culture of "complacency" to one of empowerment.

In 1995 NPR II (Executive Office of the President, 1995) set out to implement four new management improvement themes within the federal cabinet agencies. These included: (1) consolidating federal categorical programs, (2) devolving more program authority to state and local governments, (3) privatizing federal activities, and (4) terminating numerous federal programs and agencies. The impact of these initiatives was to be a more vigorous agency culture.

The Clinton Administration now reports that NPR I and II have transformed the federal government (Gore, 1996), producing a savings of $118.9 billion since 1993.1 York (1996), in an article analyzing the results of NPR, concurs with Gore's 1996 progress report. York found that the NPR eliminated 156,900 federal positions from 1993 through 1996.

In an article, which compared "reinventing government" to efforts in the private sector, Siegel (1996) evaluates the features of Clinton's NPR program. Siegel shows how the NPR attempts to give front line employees and managers more autonomy. Agencies were encouraged to establish hundreds of "reinvention laboratories" to experiment with new ways of conducting program business. From the "reinvention labs" and employee involvement efforts numerous "service delivery" improvements were produced. For example, the 10,000 page Federal Personnel Manual was eliminated. The NPR targeted reducing the 6,000 pages of Federal Acquisitions Regulations (FAR), which was perceived as a barrier to agency management productivity. By 1996 the Gore Report (1996) claimed that the NPR helped facilitate the elimination of "thousands of pages" of procurement regulations within the federal cabinet agencies. In addition the Congress passed a NPR recommended law that would further streamline federal procurement regulations (the Federal Acquisition Reform Act).

Kettl (1994) supports Siegel's findings on the results of the NPR. In addition to the Federal Personnel Manual, the Standard Form 171 was eliminated. The Office of Management (OPM) to free up agency official decision -making issued also new "waivers". Kettl believes that the major assumption behind these results is that the NPR has awarded agency employees and managers more autonomy and decision-making.

This book examines whether the results reported by Gore (1996); Siegel (1996) and Kettl (1994) actually led to changes in agency culture. This book is written as both a case and research methodology for management/research practitioners. Survey data was used to measure the degree to which federal agency employees perceive such "cultural" change within their organization and work group

The U.S. Merit Systems Protection Board (MSPB) conducts a bi-annual random survey of over 10,000 employees on issues relating to work satisfaction and agency culture. Using this data across time (1992-1996) I

---

1 The total savings is derived from three sources. First, $73.4 billion in savings from implementing the recommendations of NPRI. Second, $24 billion in savings from additional recommendations in NPRII. And third, more than $21.5 billion in savings from agency reinvention efforts beyond the recommendations of NPR I and II. (Gore 1996,1)

determined the extent to which employees perceive organizational culture change in the 21 federal cabinet agencies. Also interviews were conducted with NPR and MSPB staff to examine the extent to which they see the organizational culture of the 21 federal cabinet agencies changing since the introduction of the National Performance Review project.

An Overview of the National Reform Commission Movement

Prior to the NPR there existed a rich history, both in theory and practice, in the area of government agency reform. The "code words" reorganization and reform symbolize a general frustration with government bureaucracy. In their 1983 article, "Organizing Political Life: What Administrative Reorganization Tells Us About Government," March and Olsen did an in-depth review of the twelve administrative reorganization/reform commissions implemented at the national level since the turn of the century. March and Olsen conclude that these efforts were nothing more than "administrative rhetoric."

March and Olsen believed that this "rhetoric" was embedded in the language of the early reform commissions (the Commission on Department Methods, chaired by Charles L. Keep in 1905; the President's Commission on Economy and Efficiency, chaired by Frederick A. Cleveland in 1912; the President's Committee on Administrative Management, or Brownlow Report, 1937; and the 1949 Hoover Commission report).

The rhetoric of the early commissions emphasized "... economy and control. They speak of offices that could be abolished, salaries that could be reduced, positions that could be eliminated, and expenses that could be curtailed" (March and Olsen 1983,282-283). To many these early commissions were the by-product of the traditional management paradigm as established in the writings of Wilson (1887), Goodnow (1900), Taylor (1911), and Gulick and Urwick (1937).

Woodrow Wilson's 1887 essay, "Study of Administration," is viewed as the academic forerunner of the traditional management model. Wilson believed that as America entered a new industrial era, government would need a "science of study" to meet the new administrative challenge. He believed that the complex problems of society, and a maturing democracy demanded a systematic study of administration. Wilson urged that administration within the public sector adopt a more scientific posture for its operations.

According to Wilson administration is "government in action." In his essay Wilson criticizes contemporary thought as being centered in "constitutional" as opposed to administrative analysis. Wilson believed that government's tendency to "follow the whims of a court" would now shift to "follow the views of the nation" (1887,362). According to Wilson the time had arrived for American scholars to examine concepts of administration. Wilson believed that the intellectual community lagged behind Europe ("Many nations are ahead of us in organization and administrative skill," Wilson 1887,367).

Wilson believed that government could be reformed through principles of administration.

"This is why there should be a science of administration which shall seek to straighten the paths of government... to strengthen and purify its organization." (1887,363)

Also Wilson believed that:

"It is the object of administrative study to discover what government... can do... and do these proper things with the utmost possible efficiency... it would rescue executive methods from the confusion and costliness of empirical experiment." (1887,359)

Within the decade, Wilson's call for greater administrative efficiency emerged in the early presidential reorganization commissions. In 1905, Charles H. Keep chaired the first national commission of the century. The Keep Commission echoed Wilson (1887) and Goodnow's (1900) call to improve administrative efficiency. According to Kraines (1970) the Keep Commission sought to decentralize the executive branch, with agency control by the Congress.

By 1911 Taylor's principles of scientific management emerged as a pure systems approach to the study of organizations. Through the scientific method he attempted to develop managerial knowledge. This managerial knowledge was used to achieve maximum individual and organizational efficiency. According to Taylor the art of management is "knowing exactly what you want men to do, and then seeing that they do it in the best and cheapest way." (Taylor 1903,21)

Through the early 1930s the rational management model continued to dominate as the prevailing management theory of the time. In their comprehensive essay on the history of organizational culture, Ouchi and Wilkins (1985) found that the mainstream writers on culture sought "to discover the rational basis of organizational life." (Ouchi and Wilkins 1985,464) Ouchi and Wilkins acknowledged Gulick and Urwick's 1937 Papers on the Science of Administration as providing the core theory in administrative rationality. Many view Gulick and Urwick's essay as a landmark in the field of public administration. It emphasized the study of the formal organizational structure, and the application of scientific principles (Planning, Organizing, Staffing, Directing, Coordinating, Reporting and Budgeting - POSDCRB).

By 1937 the rational management model reached its watershed mark with the President's Committee on Administrative Management (The Brownlow

Report). The Brownlow Report speaks directly to the values and theories of Wilson and the traditional management paradigm. (Goodnow 1900; Taylor 1903 and 1911; Willoughby 1927; White 1933; Gulick and Urwick, 1937) The Brownlow Report recommended ways to improve the administrative efficiency of the federal government by centralizing personnel policy under the President's control. It also sought to legitimize the President's authority to reorganize the federal cabinet agencies.

The tone and philosophy of the traditional management paradigm continued with each national commission that followed the Brownlow Report. In its first report to President Truman, the Hoover Commission (1949) argued that, "we must first reorganize the executive branch to give it simplicity of structure." (Hoover Report 1949,viii). The objective of the Hoover Report was to "establish a clear line of control from the President to department and agency heads." (Hoover Report 1949,7-8)

As the reform movement took hold in state government, one can see parallel themes to the federal reform effort. State government reform echoed traditional management's belief that power should be centralized in the chief executive. In his review of state executive branch reorganizations (1965 through 1987) Conant found that the "centralization of power" trend was clearly linked to the writings of Wilson and Brownlow.

Today many writers take a different view on the role of "centralized authority" in the reform movement. For example, Arnold (1995) argues that the Hoover Commission was the last commission to centralize the bureaucracy and strengthen the executive powers of the President.

March, Olsen and Conant differ from this perspective. They do not believe that traditional management's influence ended with the Hoover report. These writers conclude, that after eight decades, the reform movement continues to emphasize the need for a strong executive branch, with a hierarchical system of accountability. Moe (1994) also believes that the influence of the traditional management paradigm continued through 1992. Moe argues that the NPR project signifies the first important departure from the traditional management paradigm.

In order to study the problem of changing government culture we must ask: what has a century of reform accomplished? March and Olsen's answer to this question is "not much." According to March and Olsen, "the history of administrative reorganization in the twentieth century is a history of rhetoric." (March and Olsen 1983,282) Hence "reorganizations tend to become collections of solutions looking for problems, ideologues looking for soapboxes, pet projects looking for supporters, and people looking for jobs." (1983,286) Accordingly, if future reform efforts are to obtain results, long-range commitment and perseverance is needed.

An examination of the national commissions that followed the Hoover

Reports supports a thesis of more rhetoric than result. In propounding the purpose of his Council on Government Organization, led by Roy Ash (Arnold, 1986; Hoff, 1994), Richard Nixon stated that restoring confidence in government would "require us to give more profound and critical attention to the question of government organization." (Nathan 1975,134) Eventually the Ash Council report was to recommend the consolidation of the major executive cabinet departments into four departments. Yet the Congress would not support its recommendations.

Five years after the Ash Council's report, President Jimmy Carter promised to "bring the horrible bureaucratic mess under control." (Moe 1994,49) Through executive order, the President's Reorganization Project (PRP) was created in the Office and Management and Budget. (Arnold 1995) By 1979 the President's Reorganization Project (1977-1980) was "dead in the water." Like its predecessor, the PRP's attempt to reorganize the federal government from the "top-down and bottom-up" could not win Congressional support.

In 1982, the Reagan Administration initiated the President's Private Sector Survey on Cost Control, chaired by businessman J. Peter Grace. The Grace Commission issued 47 public reports containing 2,478 recommendations. (Goodsell 1984) According to Arnold the major recommendations of the Grace Commission found little support for adoption, yet for "quite different reasons" than the Nixon and Carter effort. In Arnold's words, "the Grace Commission recommendations failed, perhaps, because they were really intended to castigate government and not change it." (Arnold 1995,413)

Caiden's (1991) view on the failures of the national reform commissions of the 1970s and 1980s differs from that of Arnold. According to Caiden the trends of these commissions often reflected the views of a "managerial elite" of government outsiders whose agenda was at odds with the bureaucracy. According to Caiden these outsiders sought high performance standards, setting the bureaucracy "free to manage, to set objectives, to set priorities." (Caiden 191,122)

In their review of attempts to reform government, Lance (1977), March and Olsen (1983), Meier (1980), and Morgan and Pelissero (1980) are hard pressed to prove that government reform improved the efficiency and effectiveness of government. In the end the rhetoric of reform exceeded any benefits.

However More (1994) and Schachter (1997) suggest that public administration may have entered a new era called the "post progressive" period. Caiden (1991) also speaks to the challenges of this new era; that successful change in government begins with the development of a work culture where talent is nurtured and motivated. Moe and Schachter suggest that the NPR principles of "reinvention" signal a dramatic shift away from the traditional management paradigm. This departure occurs in two ways.

First, the NPR seeks to make government more responsive by eliminating red tape. Second, the NPR creates an atmosphere where the mission of the federal agencies would be "customer driven." This book attempts to measure these changes associated with the Clinton Administration's reinventing government strategy (the National Performance Review).

Chapter 2

Review of the Literature

The Roots of the NPR

Osborne and Gaebler (1992) supply the theoretical and conceptual roots of the National Performance Review. In their 1992 text, *Reinventing Government: How the Entrepreneurial Spirit is Transforming the Public Sector from Schoolhouse to State House, City Hall to Pentagon*, Osborne and Gaebler outlined a cultural and behavioral shift in the management of government away from bureaucracy toward an entrepreneurial government.

The shift toward an entrepreneurial government is premised on "ten principles for entrepreneurial government" (e.g., entrepreneurial governments are customer driven). When these principles are fully implemented, government becomes "reinvented." (Osborne and Gaebler 1992) In many respects reinventing government attempts to integrate the fair market/privatization literature of the 1970's and 1980's (including Public Choice theory), and the business/management literature of Drucker (1968), Peters and Waterman (1982), and Kanter-Moss (1983).

Many of the principles of Reinventing Government (improvement of quality, empowerment of employees to solve organizational problems) are based on the TQM (Total Quality Management) approach used extensively by the private and public sector in the 1980s. Balk, Bouckaert and Bronner (1989) question whether TQM accomplished its goals after a decade of implementation. According to Balk et al., "the difficulty is, on the one hand, to accept the necessity for hierarchial structure but then, on the other, to engage in strategic relaxation of the usual authority norms when this enhances creative thought from lower levels." (Balk, Bouckaert, and Bronner 1989,410)

In examining NPR's results, James Carroll (1995) reaches a similar conclusion. Carroll believes that as an administrative theory the NPR is "driven by budgetary politics." Regarding NPR's goal to create a "customer driven" culture in the federal government, Carroll believes that this NPR principle is inconsistent with "most federal responsibilities and functions." NPR's impact must be limited.

In many respects Mel Dubnick's 1994 essay, "Coup Against King Bureaucracy" may explain the difficulties that Balk et al., and Carroll allude to in reshaping the "bureaucratic" structure. Dubnick reviewed the various reform periods that marked this century. Dubnick believed that the bureaucratic paradigm will continue to "thrive as the conventional wisdom in public administration" in spite of the change strategies that TQM or Reinventing Government seek (1994, 269). Dubnick's premise is supported by March and Olsen's findings that the reform efforts of the twentieth century have become an exercise in administrative rhetoric. For the most part, public institutions remain unchanged. In their 1997 textbook, *Transforming the Bureaucracy*, Osborne and Plastrik address this dilemma. They believe a central issue facing today's public organization is how the prevailing bureaucratic model can be transformed into an entrepreneurial-bottom up culture. They argue such a cultural shift is critical to the public organization's ability to survive, adapt and change within the current climate of less government.

This book seeks to add some empirical evidence to evaluating the extent to which Dubnick's or Carroll's premise is justified. An examination is made of the federal cabinet agencies to determine if the NPR has changed their culture in specified ways consonant with reinventing government's particular philosophy. The remainder of Chapter 2 examines what reinventing government and the NPR mean by public organization change. We can then look at some empirical evidence showing whether shifts in these areas have occurred under NPR.

Transforming the Bureaucracy

One of the conclusions of the "reinventing government" literature is that public organizations need to reform both the structures and systems which constrain human and organizational performance in public institutions. Once these structures and systems are "let go," the public sector work force will evolve into a higher state of knowledge, discipline, and accountability. (Osborne and Gaebler 1992; Caiden 1992; Brady and Woller 1994; Gore 1993; Thompson 1993; Ban and Riccucci 1993)

Throughout *Reinventing Government*, Osborne and Gaebler argue that the bureaucratic organization is at an important crossroad of change. They have the reader believing that the voting public, elective representatives, and the civil servant await anxiously at these crossroads.

Reinventing government, "is for those who care about government-because they work in government, or work with government, or study government, or simply want their governments to be more effective" (xv).

Within the Gore report (NPR I) five strategies are recommended to improve the effectiveness of the federal agencies. Each of these strategies seeks to transform the traditional bureaucratic model as we know it. These are:

"First, we will streamline the budget process, to remove the manifold restrictions that consume managers' time and literally force them to waste money... Second, we will decentralize personnel policy, to give managers the tools they need to manage effectively-the authority to hire promote, reward, and fire... Third, we will streamline procurement, to reduce the enormous waste built into the process we use to buy $200 billion a year in goods and service... Fourth, we will reorient the inspectors general, to shift their focus from punishing those who violate rules and regulations to helping agencies learn to perform better... Fifth, we will eliminate thousands of other regulations that hamstring federal employees, to cut the final Lilliputian ropes on the federal giant." (Gore 1993,13).

Leading within the Federal Cabinet Agencies

Osborne and Gaebler believe that the contemporary public bureaucracy's culture must be shaped by a new and different leadership. In the reinventing government model these new leaders must act as "entrepreneurs" within the public organization. According to Osborne and Gaebler these entrepreneurs employ leadership strategies that will

"Return control to those who work down where the rubber meets the road. They must use participatory management to decentralize decision making; they encourage teamwork, to overcome the rigid barriers that separate people in hierarchial institutions; they create institutional champions." (254)

Through its vision of a reinvented federal government, the Gore Task Force (1993) echoes the importance of leadership (i.e., "We must look to the nation's top leaders and managers to break ground" p.88). NPR I further outlines this new leadership vision:

"Transforming our federal government to do better will mean recasting what people do as they work... they will turn bosses into coaches, from directors into negotiators, from employees into thinkers and doers." (Gore 1993,88)

To attain this new leadership vision the Gore report offered the following recommendations:

"The President should issue a directive detailing his vision, plan, and commitment to creating quality government... Every federal department and agency should designate a chief operating officer... The President should appoint a President's Management Council to lead the quality revolution and ensure the implementation of National Performance Review Plans... The President's Management Council will launch quality management 'basic training' for all employees, starting with top officials, and cascading throughout the entire executive branch." (Gore 1993,89-90)

The theoretical foundation of how leaders affect culture is well documented in the management and organizational literature. In his classic 1938 work, *Functions of the Executive*, Chester I. Barnard argued that the executive of his time would have to create, manage and manipulate the organization's value system. Barnard believed that organizational commitment could be attained through the leader's ability to induce and persuade.

Another major work on leadership was Douglas McGregor's 1960 work, *The Human Side of the Enterprise*. McGregor made a very compelling argument for managers to adopt a more "trusting" view of their employees. He assumed that if the worker was committed to the values and goals of the organization, the manager could maintain high performance through greater delegation and input from the worker. McGregor's Theory X and Theory Y remains widely recognized in the literature.

Many contemporary writers on management and leadership echo Barnard and McGregor's earlier themes. Henry Mintzberg's managerial typology describes the many roles that a manager must fulfill within the organization. Perhaps the strongest statement in Mintzberg's 1973 book, *The Nature of Managerial Work*, was the compelling belief that in terms of the "interpersonal" role, a manager motivates through leadership.

Today's writers in management articulate the same themes as Barnard, McGregor and Mintzberg. Geier (1991) identifies six traits consistently associated with supervision and leadership: the desire to lead, ambition and energy, honesty and integrity, self-confidence, intelligence and job-relevant knowledge. Bellavita (1989) believes that today's public sector managers need to take on the role of "heros" or champions within their organization, and must make the public sector "work a little better." Arnold and Selberg (1991) believe that today's public sector leader must challenge the *status quo* of the organization in order to create change. Covey (1991) supports the belief that managers can become champions of change. According to Covey, today's leadership emerges from an individual's core ideas and feelings. Covey exhorts leaders to "change now," so that organizations can be changed and reinvented.

According to Hambrick and Mason (1984), Niehiff, Enz and Grover (1990) and Trice and Beyer (1991), the actions of top management have a major impact on an organization's culture. In three studies (Adams 1991; Raturi 1992; and Biggerstaff 1990) it was reported that leadership plays an important role in developing an organization's culture.

Relating to the role of leadership in the NPR initiative, Barr (1994) described the critical role that Vice President Al Gore played in "jump starting" NPR. According to Barr, Gore "visibly" counteracted the cynical attitudes of mid-level managers who felt that NPR would fail. This book examines changes in agency leadership as one study variable relating to actual implementation of NPR.

Putting Customers First

One of the major "reinventing" strategies expressed by Osborne and Gaebler is that today's public organization must be flexible, adaptive and responsive to the "needs" of the citizen or customer. The subject of client or "customer" relationships is long recognized in the public administration and management literature. Meier (1979) wrote of the importance of the relationship between the public "client" and the political arena. Lipsky (1980) added to Meier's "client" assumption by constructing a model that described the street-level agencies where the values and behavior of bureaucrats impacted both the administrative processes and responsiveness to the clients.

Meier and Lipsky were followed by Tom Peters and Bill Waterman's in their heralded field report, *In Search of Excellence*, (1982). Peters and Waterman studied over 80 companies, and concluded that there was a common formula for success; instill in the work force a strong sense of "customer service."

Within the NPR the influence of the "customer driven" literature emerges as a central focus in the Clinton Administration's reinvention image.   NPR I lists twenty   actions to accomplish the goal of a government more responsive to the customer (i.e making service organizations compete, creating market dynamics, use of market mechanisms).   One of the actions outlined in the report is:

> "The President should issue a directive requiring all federal agencies that deliver services to the public to create customer service programs that identify and survey customers. The order will establish the following standard for quality: Customer service equal to the best in business."
> (Gore 1993,47-48)

Inventing A New Learning Culture

In *Reinventing Government*, Osborne and Gaebler state, "What we need most if this revolution is to succeed... is a new framework for understanding a government, a new way of thinking about government." (Osborne and Gaebler 1993,321) In the National Commission on the State and Local Public Service's 1993 report this framework of understanding is referred to as the development of a new culture of a "learning government." According to Carroll (1995) the NPR sought to transform the culture of the federal agencies into one where program, front-line managers and employees could achieve results, free of staff oversight, rules and regulations.

Osborne and Gaebler's model of reinventing government outlines an organization culture characterized by participatory management, decentralized decision making and team work. The origins of Osborne and Gaebler's "team" (**p. 268**) approach to building a new culture in the public bureaucracy is Peter Drucker's *The Age of Discontinuity* (1968).   Drucker (1968) describes the importance of teams to organizations.

> "Knowledge workers still need superiors... But knowledge work itself knows no hierarchy, for there are no "higher" and "lower" knowledge. Knowledge is either relevant to a given task or irrelevant to it. The task decides, not the name, the age, or the budget of the discipline, or the rank of the individual plying it... Knowledge, therefore, has to be organized as a team in which the task decides who is in charge, when, for what, and for how long." (289-290).

The NPR goal of a "cultural change" is to create a "learning government". In this new climate within public organizations, managers take a "trust and lead" approach, having employees serve as "problem solvers and innovators."

Chapter three of NPR I identifies the important elements of a new learning culture within government. They are: decentralized power, holding employees accountable, and the creation of labor-management partnerships. According to NPR I:

> "Training too often is ad hoc and seldom linked to strategic or human resource planning... OPM will define the objective of federal training as the 'improvement of individual and organizational performance'... clarifying the purpose of training... will reinforce the need to use training to improve performance and results." (Gore 1993,80).

The report further recommends that government should: "Eliminate narrow restrictions on employee training to help develop a multi-skilled workforce." (Gore 1993,80). The research examines the presence of a "learning culture" in the 21 federal cabinet agencies within the context of employee empowerment and decision making, problem solving, teamwork, and the presence (or lack thereof) of a multi-skilled work force. The next chapter explains the empirical evidence that is used to evaluate the extent to which the time of purported NPR implementation was also a time of transforming bureaucracies, increasing leadership, putting customers first and inaugurating learning cultures.

Chapter 3

Evaluating Organizational Culture Change A Time-Based Multi Variate/Uni Variate Approach

The Research Problem Posed in this Study and Research Questions

In Chapters 1 and 2, a review of the literature on NPR shows no conclusive evidence that the National Performance Review has changed the organizational culture of the federal government. The Gore Report claims it has. Articles by public administration scholars such as Dubnick (1994) and Carroll (1995) posit reasons why certain changes may be limited. This book seeks to answer the question: has the change process set in place by the NPR been partially or fully met?

According to the literature, organizational culture signifies the prevailing attitudes and beliefs held by employees. Recent studies have used employee attitude surveys to measure organizational culture. (O'Reily et al. 1991; Chatman and Jehn 1994). Often this survey-based research will measure leadership, supervision, problem solving methods, teamwork, and other dimensions indicative of the organizational culture.

Since 1968 the Merit Systems Protection Board has administered a bi-annual employee attitude survey to randomly selected employees across the federal government. Specifically the Board survey measures agency work climate, supervisory effectiveness, merit pay issues, and the Senior Executive Service (SES) program. In an effort to answer the research question posited in this book questions and data were obtained from the Board survey administered in 1992 and 1996. Specifically questions were selected from the Board survey that directly related to the principles of reinvention (i.e., good supervision, making good use of skills and abilities, autonomy and freedom in work, and customer driven culture).

Question on freedom and independence

Bennis (1993) and Argyris (1992) both characterize innovation as giving employees the freedom and independence to carry out their work.

Argyris believed that once organization members were empowered to act independently, organizations could break out of the "single loop" way of thinking. Accordingly, question 33 ("I have independence in how I do my work," 1992 MSPB survey) and question 22 ("I have been given more flexibility in how I accomplish my work," 1996 survey) were selected as independent variables in the factor analysis model.

Question on teamwork

Throughout the literature on organization culture issues of participation, cooperation and teamwork are seen as critical to creating and sustaining an effective and productive organization culture. Osborne and Gaebler (1992) see group norms ("teamwork") as essential to creating an entrepreneurial/decisional climate in the reinvented public organization. Simon (1945) believed that by seeking cooperation, the administrator could achieve conformity between the individual and the organization in the decision making process. McGregor's (1960) Theory Y emerged from research on group norms, such as cooperation within a team (Bion and Triste, 1985). To build a constructive group, a manager needs to employ Theory Y's worker participation assumptions. Accordingly the survey question, "Cooperation and teamwork exists in my unit" (questions 15 and 19 in the 1992 and 1996 surveys), serves as the independent variable "participation and teamwork" in the factor analysis model.

Question on leadership

The role of the supervisor in "inculcating" motivation and values has been addressed in the literature since Chester I. Barnard's classic work, *The Functions of the Executive.* (1938) Barnard believed that executives should motivate through "objective inducements" and "inculcation of motives." The works of Roethlisberger and Dickson (1939), Bennis (1966, 1973), Argyris (1973, 1992, 1993), Osborne and Gaebler (1992), Oakley and Krug (1993), and Terry (1995) have echoed Barnard's belief in the role of supervision and leadership in developing an organization's culture. Accordingly, within the factor analysis research design I have selected the question, "My supervisor has good leadership/management skills" (questions 16 and 14 in the 1992 and 1996 survey respectively) as a variable in the factor analysis model.

Question on rewarding performance

The ability of the organization to reward and recognize performance was used as another independent variable in the regression model. This study variable builds on the research of Barnard (1938), Maslow (1954) and Herzberg and Synderman (1959) on the role that awards and recognition play in building a productive culture within organizations. Hence question 32 in the 1992 survey, "Awards in unit go to most deserving," and question 41b in the 1996 survey, "To what extent do you believe you have been treated fairly regarding awards," were selected as independent variables in the factor analysis model.

Question on employee skills

Within the literature the development of skills and abilities is critical to building productivity within organizations (Bennis, 1966, 1973, 1993; Argyris 1973, 1992, 1993; Drucker, 1968, and Herzberg and Synderman, 1959). Accordingly within the factor analysis model an independent variable on "employee skills" was selected, "I have skills needed to do my job" (question 16 and question 3 in the 1992 and 1996 surveys).

Questions on NPR

With regard to measuring the perceived level of change brought by the President's NPR program questions 10 through 12 were analyzed from the 1996 survey.

Question 10: "The efforts of the NPR have had a positive impact in bringing about change to government."

Question 11: "The NPR has had a positive impact on improving customer service to the public."

Question 12: "My organization has made the goals of the NPR an important priority."

Within this study these survey questions are used as explanatory (or independent) variables. The research examines the relationship of these variables to the dependent variable (organizational culture). To examine these variables and the proposed questions the research combined the statistical output of factor analysis, with structured interviews conducted with federal agency employees.

Question 1: Has the implementation of the National Performance Review program improved the organizational culture of the 21 federal cabinet agencies?

Question 2: Has "teamwork" within the federal cabinet agencies improved under the National Performance Review?

Question 3: Has the National Performance Review improved the problem solving and decision making processes within the federal cabinet agencies?

Question 4: Has federal agency leadership and supervision improved under the National Performance Review?

To answer these questions the research combined the quantitative procedures and output of factor analysis, with the "qualitative" focus interview approach. The data obtained in the focus group interviews was compared to the quantitative statistical data to answer each of the proposed research questions on organizational change.

For example, the focus interviews identified "key" agencies that have made progress in implementing the principles of NPR. In Chapters 5 and 6 I examine the quantitative data (cumulative eigenvalues, and factor and correlation patterns) generated on these "key" agencies.

Relating to the quantitative/statistical data, any positive or negative direction on the organizational culture variables "flagged" the research questions on organizational change for each of the federal cabinet agencies. Although the factor analysis results could not ascertain whether the NPR produced cultural change, it offers some evidence on the relationship of some of the organizational culture variables to each other (i.e. the relationship of rewards to servicing agency customers). However, the difference of means test produced significant data to ascertain the degree of perceived cultural change from 1992 to 1996.

The Selected Research Methodology

Since the 1970s there has been a growing interest in examining the nature of organization culture. Prior to the 1980s there appeared to be no consensus on how the topic of organizational culture could be empirically measured.

In their article, "Conceptual Issues in the Study of Innovation" Downs and Mohr (1976) asserted that there was an extreme variance (or "instability") in the body of empirical research on culture. Downs and Mohr argued that such data may inflate both the results and interpretations on organizational culture. They concluded that future research on organizational culture must go beyond the use of multivariate regression models.

Beginning in the 1980s many researchers responded to Downs and Mohr's challenge in their approach to the measurement of organizational culture (Mills, 1988; Hofstede et al.,1990; O'Reily et al.,1991; and Chatman and Jehn 1994).

Kachigan (1982) laid for the foundation for this research through his explanation and applications in the use of factor analysis. Since Kachigan's book it appears that factor analysis has emerged as an important research methodology in the study of organizational culture. For example, Hofstede et al., (1990), O'Reily et al., (1991) and Chatman and Jehn (1994) examined the widely held central values of organizational members using a questionnaire-based/factor analysis model. Hofstede et al., (1990) examined and compared the factor patterns of international firms based on dimensions of organizational culture (i.e., outcome orientation, team orientation, innovation). Using an instrument created by the authors (the Organizational Culture Profile or OCP) O'Reilly et al., (1991) compared the factor patterns of a sample of U.S. companies based on the OCP dimensions. These dimensions included innovation, stability, respect for people, an outcome and detail orientation, team orientation, and aggressiveness. Chatman and Jehn (1994) went further in their study of organizational culture by using the OCP instrument to compare the factor pattern of private and semi-private service sector industries (public accounting, general consulting, the U.S. Postal Service, and national household goods carriers). Chatham and Jehn concluded that the factors were common across firms.

Although these studies used validated measuring instruments to measure the organizational culture variables in their models, they did not examine how organizational culture changed over time. This book addresses this important methodological challenge through the uni variate and multi variate statistics used in the study.

Factor Analysis As A Tool in Assessing Change

Factor analysis is a statistical technique that can simplify data by clustering a large number of variables and cases into a smaller number of homogenous sets, creating a new concept, or dimension. Using this approach, researchers "are more likely to gain insight into the subject matter by simplifying data," according to Kachigan, (1982,238). Hence, factor analysis will reduce a large set of study variables into a smaller, more manageable and interpretable number of factors. As a research approach, factor analysis is used to discover patterns (or common factors) which underlie a set of independent predicator (factor input) variables. As Figure 1 illustrates, each of the arrows from a common factor to a variable is identified with a coefficient (i.e., for b21 variable 2 is shown as emerging from factor 1). These coefficients represent factor loadings, which are correlations between factors emerging from the factor analysis and the study variables.

Figure 3-1

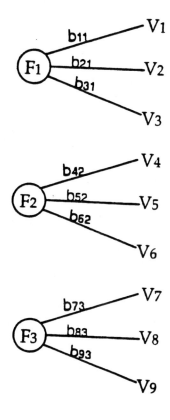

In my examination of the NPR, factor analysis and difference of means test results were used to examine the variance attributed to study variables vis-a-vis the research questions.

The Research Methodology

This study on the NPR attempted to add to the literature by comparing "shifts" in the organization culture from two sets of data (the 1992 and 1996 MSPB surveys). Principal factor analysis and the difference of means test was performed on two sets of data (the Merit System Protection Board's 1992 and 1996 survey) to answer the proposed research question (Had the culture of the federal cabinet agencies changed?).

Each of the six cultural study variables selected in the study related to the principles of reinventing government: three questions from the survey measure levels of supervisory and management effectiveness (Q13, Q15 and Q17 in 1992; Q14, Q15 and Q16 in 1996); one question measures organizational teamwork (Q 20 in 1992 and Q19 in 1996); two questions measure employee skill and knowledge utilization (Q3 and Q4 in 1992; Q3 and Q13 in 1996); two questions relate to employee performance management, including recognition and reward systems (Q33 and Q39B in 1992; and Q41B and Q61C in 1996); and, two questions measure worker autonomy and freedom, and the presence of a "customer driven" culture in the federal cabinet agencies (Q23 and Q32 in 1992 and Q11 and Q22 in 1996).

Data Sources Used

Since 1968 The Federal Merit Systems Protection Board has surveyed, on a bi-annual basis, employees in the major federal cabinet agencies. The Merit Systems Protection Board's bi-annual survey (Appendix A) is designed to collect facts and statements of attitude and opinion on a number of personnel/human resource management issues including pay, working conditions, and the quality of supervisors, coworkers and job applicants. Although the MSPB survey was designed to address overall levels of job satisfaction among groups of federal employees, a number of questions in the survey measure the employee's perception of organizational or agency culture. These survey questions form the basis for the study variables examined in this book. For the most part, similar survey questions were used as study variables in the study on organizational culture by Chatman and Jehn (1994) and O'Reilly et al., (1991).

The four sections of the survey include:
Part I.   All Employees
Part II.   Supervisors
Part III.   Senior Executive Service
Part IV.   Personal and Job Information

Using a random sampling strategy, the Merit System Protection Board sampled 20,851 federal employees in 1992; 13,432 employees responded to the survey. In the 1996 survey 9,710 employees responded. The observational data collected in the study was drawn from attitudinal data in the "All Employees" part of the survey. Attitudes are measured via a Likert scale to assess employee attitudes towards personnel and human resource issues. The scale used in the Merit Board's survey ranges from 1-5 (strongly agree, agree, neither agree nor disagree, disagree, strongly disagree, don't know/can't judge).

Measures

In their study of the organizational culture of eight firms, Chatman and Jehn (1994) used the results of a factor analysis to examine whether the Organizational Culture Profile (OCP) questions loaded above .30 on one of seven distinct factors. Chatman and Jehn compared these results to the factor structure findings reported by O'Reilly et al., (1991) who used the same organizational culture survey in their study of culture.

The approach taken in the study of the NPR contrasts differently from this research on organization culture. Difference of means test results were compared to the factor loading patterns on the ten questions used to measure organizational culture change.

The Merit Board survey uses a Likert scale of 1 through 5 (i.e., strongly agree to strongly disagree) to measure employee perceptions. If the difference in the mean score between 1992 and 1996 has a value of 0 or less, the respondents more strongly agree on the questions relating to supervisory and management effectiveness.

Step one observes the difference in means (DFM) for Q13, 15 and Q17 in 1992 to Q14, Q15 and Q16 in 1996 and determine if the mean value difference for each question is less than 0. This is represented by the following formula:

DFM $_{Q13,Q14}$ = M$_{Q13,t1}$ - $_{MQ14,t2}$
DFM $_{Q15,Q15}$ = M$_{Q15,t1}$ - $_{MQ15,t2}$
DFM $_{Q17,Q16}$ = M$_{Q17,t1}$ - $_{MQ16,t2}$

If DFM $\leq$ 0, respondents more strongly agree on the supervisory cultural question.

Step 2. The "t" value in the difference in means were "flagged" when the obtained value for the cultural question was less than 0.

A "t" value between .05 and .005 qualifies rejection of the null hypothesis (no change on how employees perceived this particular question on agency culture). This allows acceptance of the proposition that there is a significant "mean" difference on this cultural question over time (1992 through 1996). This procedure is explained by the following formula:

The value of T for the question, "Supervisor is a leader" = $T_{Q13,t1,Q14,t2}$
The value of T for the question, "Supervisor is organizes group effectively" = $T_{Q15,t1,Q15,t2}$
The value of T for the question, "I am satisfied with my supervisor" = $T_{Q16,t1,Q17,t2}$

Step 3. For the question "Supervisor is a leader" if $T_{Q13,t1,Q14,t2}$ is $\geq$ .01, then the research question is supported.

Step 4. For the question "Supervisor organizes group effectively" = $T_{Q15,t1,Q15,t2}$ is $\geq$ .01, then the research question is supported.

Step 5. For the question "I am satisfied with my supervisor" = $T_{Q16,t1,Q17,t2}$ is $\geq$ .01, then the research question is supported.

6. Step 2 was applied to the remaining variables or questions used to assess culture.

Comparing the Difference in Means and Factor Analysis Test Results

For the 21 cabinet agencies I then examined how the ten cultural questions correlated within the common factor over time. In this procedure the correlation coefficients (factor loadings) were examined for each question by agency. This latter procedure departs significantly from the research done by Chatman and Jehn and O'Reilly et al. Unlike the approach taken by Chatman and Jehn and O'Reilly, et al., the NPR study examined how the cultural questions loaded to each other across-time.

For example, the loadings for the "reward system" questions (Q33 and

Q39B in 1992) and the customer service question (Q in 1992) were examined with respect to each other. If the direction of the factor loadings for the customer service and reward questions was inverse in 1992, and positive and direct in 1996, I concluded that there may be a stronger linkage between agency rewards and servicing the customer (a desired NPR outcome). Likewise if the opposite occurred (i.e., the question loadings were inverse to each other in both 1992 and 1996) I concluded that there was no change in linking awards to customer service over time. These results were then compared to the difference of means test to answer the research question.

Chapter 4

Interview Results Focus Meetings with NPR Staff

In March, 1997 four interviews were conducted with two current members of Vice President Gore's National Performance Review Project, one former member of the NPR project, and a research analyst from the U.S. Merit System's Protection Board (the focus interviews are found in Appendix B of this dissertation). The purpose of these interviews was to identify specific federal agencies that have made progress in implementing the strategies of reinventing government and the National Performance Review. The NPR staff serve in an advisory capacity to the "line" federal agencies in implementing the principles of NPR.

One major advantage to the agency interviews is that they steered the interpretation of quantitative data obtained in the factor analysis. A second advantage is that the interviews allowed me to go "beyond" the meaning of the quantitative data. The interviews provided the basis to explore the meaning of organizational culture change in the federal cabinet agencies as shown in the factor analysis output.

A primary disadvantage to using interview data with NPR staff is that this organization may have its own "bias" in order to "save face" for the Vice President's initiative. Some of the questions posed to NPR staff were:

1.   How has the NPR changed the organizational structure of the 21 federal cabinet agencies? In which agencies have you noticed the greatest change in organizational structure?

2.   In relationship to the NPR goal of decentralized decision making, which agencies have driven decision making down to the lowest employee level?

3.   In which agencies has there been the most visible leadership in support of the NPR?

4.   Is there a noticeable change in the skills and knowledge of the federal worker? In which agencies have you noticed such change?

5.   According to Osborne and Gaebler, the "reinventing" manager

uses participative management to accomplish the goals of reinventing government.   To what extent has participatory management taken hold in the federal agencies under NPR?

6. Reinventing government develops rewards and incentive systems which will make government more "customer" oriented.   Which agencies have invested the most in the development of such reward and incentive systems?

Table 4-1 summarizes the responses to these questions in a matrix format.   The table illustrates each agency reported in the interviews against the proposed five organizational culture variables.

Table 4-1. Cultural Change As Reported in Focus Interviews

Agencies with reported change	Freedom/ Independence	Leadership	Rewards/ Performance	Good use of skills	Customer Service
HUD	X	X			
FEMA	X	X		X	X
HHS	X	X			X
VA	X				
Agriculture			X		
Education			X		
Labor			X		
OPM	X				X

Focus Interview Results

During the interviews, NPR staff reported that there was no evidence to suggest overall cultural change within the federal executive agencies. This same conclusion is supported by the factor analysis and difference of means test procedures (Chapters 5 and 6) performed on the cultural questions for each of the 21 cabinet agencies in the study time series.

In the focus interviews the NPR staff noted a few high spots with respect to cultural change in five of the federal agencies. This change occurred for the cultural questions relating to freedom/independence, leadership, skill usage, rewards/performance, and customer service. The five agencies where there was reported change include the Federal Emergency Management Agency (FEMA), the Department of Health and Human Services (HHS), the Department of Housing and Urban Development (HUD), and the Office of Personnel Management (OPM).

In the interviews the NPR staff believed that the Department of Health and Human Services had transformed itself into a highly decentralized organization comprised of "self managed" work teams. In the words of one NPR staffer, HHS's Social Security Administration developed a strong "team leader" organizational structure, with "front end supervisors serving as team leaders." In contrast to these conclusions, the results of the difference of means test (Chapter 6) presents a different perspective on how HHS changed from 1992 to 1996. For example, the difference of means test performed on the question "I have independence in how I do my work" shows the average response decreasing from 2.28 to 2.96 at a .005 level of significance. For the HHS employee this could mean that respondents perceive having less flexibility in their jobs from 1992 to 1996.

Also the results of the difference of means test performed on other cultural questions for HHS support rejection of the null hypothesis (no difference in how employees view culture). This occurred on the reward, skills, and customer service questions at a .005 level of significance. The fact that HHS employees see less cultural change on these four questions and, at a .005 level of significance, could mean that the mass of HHS employees do not see the change as reported by the NPR. Perhaps this difference is attributed to how the NPR staff views change vis-a-vis the mass of HHS employees. For example the NPR staff were impressed by the role that HHS management played in the change process. In contrast the difference of means test performed on the role of managers shows that there is no significant difference in how HHS staff perceives HHS management.

For the Office of Personnel Management a similar contrast was found on the focus interviews and the quantitative data. In the focus interviews NPR believed that OPM transformed a major segment of its investigatory mission into an Employee Stock Ownership Plan (ESOP). According to NPR staff this change has awarded employees more power and decision making authority. Siegel (1996) and Kettl (1994) also cite

OPM's massive "streamlining" effort to reduce bureaucratic red tape, empowering OPM employees to serve more as "consultants" to their constituencies and clients. According to Siegel, (1996) OPM eliminated the Federal Personnel Manual, the "dreaded all in one" Standard Form 171. Kettl (1994), in his appraisal of the NPR, reported a major OPM initiative to delegate personnel decision making authority to the federal agencies.

In contrast to these opinions on the OPM, the results of the difference of means test presents a different view. For example, the difference of means test performed on the question "I have independence in how I do my work" shows that the average response to this question decreased from 2.12 to 2.77 at a .005 level of significance. For OPM employees this could mean that they have less flexibility in their jobs from 1992 to 1996.

Also in OPM the results of the difference of means test on the rewards and customer service questions supports rejection of the null hypothesis (no difference in how employees view culture) at a .005 level of significance. Also the difference of means test for the question "my supervisor is organized," and "I am satisfied with my supervisor" supports rejection of the null hypothesis at a .005 and .01 level of significance.

In contrast to OPM and HHS the difference of means test may support the NPR view that job independence changed in the Department of Housing and Urban Development. For example, the NPR staff report that HUD has transformed agency decision making downward "through a significant reduction in management positions." In comparing this finding to the difference of means test, the null hypothesis was not rejected for the question "I have independence in how I do my work." Although we cannot conclude that HUD employees have more independence, the results of the difference of means test may suggest that decision making may have changed in HUD.

Finally in the Departments of Agriculture, Education and Labor the NPR staff report change in each agency's performance management system. Within these three agencies a new "360" degree performance management plan was developed. However, when comparing this observed change to the difference of means test for the question "I am treated fairly in awards," the null hypothesis was rejected. From this data I conclude that employees perceive less fairness in awards from 1992 to 1996 within these three agencies. The data suggest that certain structural changes that seem important as change harbingers to NPR staff may not change agency culture as perceived by the mass of agency employees.

Chapter 5: Factor Analysis

In their study of the organizational culture of eight firms, Chatman and Jehn (1994) used the results of a factor analysis to examine whether the Organizational Culture Profile (OCP) questions loaded above .30 on one of seven distinct factors. Chatman and Jehn compared these results to the factor structure findings reported by O'Reilly et al., (1991) who used the same organizational culture survey in their study of culture.

In this research a somewhat different approach is taken in contrast to Chatman and Jehn's and O'Reilly, et al's approach. First, I have examined the entire set of eigenvalues over time to test the efficacy of the cultural questions. One result derived from the entire set of eigenvalues found in Table 5-1 is that the efficacy of the organizational culture questions decreased in a majority of the federal cabinet agencies (19). This finding leads me to conclude that the variance of the population being surveyed is explained less by the cultural questions than in 1992.

A second way in which this researh differs from the approach taken by Chatman and Jehn and O'Reilly, et al. is in the examination of how the cultural questions load on the distinct factors. For example, I found that 18 of the 21 federal agencies show a reduction in the number of cultural questions which load at .30 and above for the distinct factors within those agencies. In the remaining four agencies (OPM, Treasury, the Small Business Administration and the Department of the Navy) the factor loadings increased or remained constant to the distinct factors. For each of these agencies there are distinct patterns on how the "reward system" (Q33 and Q39B in 1992) and the customer service questions (Q in 1992) load with respect to each other in 1992. Unlike the approach taken by Chatman and Jehn and O'Reilly, et al., I will compare how these and other cultural questions load to each other across time. From this analysis I can see how culture has changed during the NPR implementation period. For example, if the direction of the factor loadings for the customer service and reward questions were inverse in 1992, and positive and direct in 1996, I would conclude that there may be a strong linkage between agency rewards and servicing the customer (a desired NPR outcome). Likewise, if the opposite occurred (i.e., the question loadings were inverse to each other in 1992 and 1996), we can assume that no change occurred in linking awards to servicing the customer in 1996. In Chapter 6 this pattern will be compared to the difference of means test. The difference of means test will measure concurrence on how employees see the agency's award system during the NPR time period.

TABLE 5-1 Cumulative Eigenvalues for 21 Federal Cabinet Agencies, 1992-1996

	1992		1996			
AGENCY	**NSF**	**CE**	**NSF**	**CE**	**DCE**	**Ho1:Proved DCE>0**
Agriculture	2	0.53	2	0.5	-0.03	No
Commerce	3	0.65	3	0.6	-0.05	No
Air Force	3	0.64	3	0.61	-0.03	No
Army	2	0.53	2	0.5	-0.03	No
Navy	3	0.65	3	0.6	-0.05	No
Education	2	0.58	3	0.62	0.04	**Yes**
Energy	2	0.54	2	0.49	-0.05	No
EPA	3	0.62	3	0.59	-0.03	No
GSA	3	0.66	3	0.62	-0.04	No
HHS	3	0.63	2	0.51	-0.12	No
HUD	3	0.64	3	0.61	-0.03	No
Interior	3	0.63	2	0.52	-0.11	No
Justice	3	0.67	3	0.61	-0.06	No
LABOR	3	0.64	3	0.59	-0.05	No
NASA	3	0.66	3	0.59	-0.07	No
OPM	3	0.62	3	0.63	0	Yes
SBA	3	0.62	3	0.59	-0.03	No
DOT	3	0.63	2	0.5	-0.13	No
Treasury	3	0.63	3	0.59	-0.04	No
State	3	0.64	3	0.6	-0.04	No
VA	3	0.65	3	0.61	-0.04	No

In analyzing the factor pattern structure of the Small Business Administration (Table 5-2) dimension three contains a positive loading of .69 for "Unit customers are satisfied with quality", and a negative loading of -.47 for the question "I have been treated fairly on awards." For the Department of Treasury, (Table 5-3) the third dimension "Unit customers are satisfied with quality" loads at .45, while "Awards in unit go to the most deserving" and "I have been treated fairly on awards" have negative loadings of -.54 and -.63. For the Department of Navy (Table 5-5) a similar pattern occurs; the third dimension contains a positive loading of .45 for "Unit customers are satisfied with quality" and a negative loading for "Awards in unit go to the most deserving" (-.50) and "I have been treated on awards" (-.61). Finally for OPM (Table 5-5) the third dimension contains a positive loading (.40) on the question, "I have independence in how I do my work", and negative loadings on "Awards in unit go to the most deserving" (-.54) and "I have been treated on awards" (-.56). This research will address how these factor loadings changed in 1996 for the Departments of Treasury, Navy, the Office of Personnel Management and the Small Business Administration (Tables 5-2 through 5-5). I will also examine the factor pattern structure of five other cabinet agencies where I found directional relationships between the cultural questions over time Tables 5-6 through 5-10). For the remaining 12 agencies (Tables 5-11 to 5-22 in the chapter appendix) no directional relationship between the cultural questions was observed in the factor pattern structure.

Factor Pattern Structure - 1992

A review of the factor pattern structure for the 1992 data shows that "customer service" is inversely related to the merit award questions in the Environmental Protection Agency (EPA) and the Departments of Housing and Urban Development (HUD), State, Treasury, Transportation and the Small Business Administration (SBA). For EPA (Table 5-6) the second dimension contains a positive loading of .69 for "unit customers are satisfied with quality," and a negative loading for "I have been treated fairly on awards" (-.44). For HUD (Table 5-7) in 1992 dimension three contains a positive loading of .20 for "unit customers are satisfied with quality", while "I have been treated fairly in awards" has a negative loading of -.61. In the Treasury Department (Table 5-3) dimension three contained a positive loading for "unit

Table 5-2.

Small Business Administration	1992			1996		
	Factor 1	Factor 2	Factor 3	Factor 1	Factor 2	Factor 3
I have the skills I need to do my job	0.21081	0.50712	0.45358	0.02304	0.46312	0.8095
Job makes good use of my skills and abilities	0.51335	0.35572	0.07442	****	****	.0946
(Organization makes good use of my skills and abilities)	****	****	****	0.62682	0.3013	****
Immediate supervisor has good leadership skills	0.84735	-0.35662	****	****	****	****
(My supervisor has good management skills)	****	****	****	0.86599	-0.25619	.1259
Immediate supervisor organized group effectively	0.79304	-0.40414	****	****	****	****
(Supervisor has organized work effectively)	****	****	****	0.84395	-0.23778	.1283
Overall, I'm satisfied with my supervisor	0.85295	-0.29875	0.01766	0.86496	-0.3012	.1020
Cooperation and teamwork exist in unit	0.68253	-0.01222	0.10283	0.5609	0.16764	0.11377
(Spirit of cooperation exists in work unit)	****	****	****	****	****	****
Unit customers are satisfied with quality	****	-0.04238	0.69152	****	****	****
Awards in unit go to the most deserving	****	0.28109	-0.36005	****	****	****
(My organization promotes on relative ability)	****	****	****	0.41143	0.47867	-0.1197
I have been treated fairly in awards	0.60116	0.38258	-0.47231	0.48704	0.06403	-0.4333
I have independence in how I do my work	0.46242	0.41694	0.1529	****	****	****
(I have more flexibility in the last two years)	****	****	****	0.62988	0.04432	****
NPR had improved customer service	****	****	****	0.23765	0.56155	****
Eigenvalue	3.995	1.1646	1.0786	3.7781	1.0968	1.0606
Difference	2.8303	0.086	0.2028	2.6813	0.0362	0.1783
Proportion	0.3995	0.1165	0.1079	0.3778	0.1097	0.1061
Cumulative	0.3995	0.516	0.6238	0.3778	0.4875	0.5936

Table 5-3.

Treasury Department	1992			1996		
	Factor 1	Factor 2	Factor 3	Factor 1	Factor 2	Factor 3
I have the skills I need to do my job	0.2548	0.4593	0.43622	0.16587	0.17316	0.75616
Job makes good use of my skills and abilities	0.57987	0.46726	0.09717	****	****	****
(Organization makes good use of my skills and abilities)	****	****	****	0.51274	0.50514	0.15895
Immediate supervisor has good leadership skills	0.79664	-0.46577	0.07614	****	****	****
(My supervisor has good management skills)	****	****	****	0.85952	-0.36213	-0.03054
Immediate supervisor organized group effectively	0.76905	-0.46057	0.10213	****	****	****
(Supervisor has organized work effectively)	****	****	****	0.86184	-0.27301	0.0494
Overall, I'm satisfied with my supervisor	0.81765	-0.40558	0.0649	0.8674	-0.34656	-0.02125
Cooperation and teamwork exist in unit	0.61779	0.06142	0.17578	****	****	****
(Spirit of cooperation exists in work unit)	****	****	****	0.57015	0.14352	-0.02102
Unit customers are satisfied with quality	0.37478	0.29616	0.44974	****	****	****
Awards in unit go to the most deserving	0.58962	0.25874	-0.54276	****	****	****
(My organization promotes on relative ability)	****	****	****	0.24382	0.50857	-0.47917
I have been treated fairly in awards	0.52958	0.24432	-0.62862	0.39768	0.39838	-0.40687
I have independence in how I do my work	0.53973	0.44099	0.02968	****	****	****
(I have more flexibility in the last two years)	****	****	****	0.51259	0.23005	0.08603
NPR had improved customer service	****	****	****	0.13653	0.56579	0.30547
Eigenvalue	3.7373	1.4355	1.144	3.3484	1.4219	1.0972
Difference	2.3019	0.2915	0.2717	1.9265	0.3247	0.1541
Proportion	0.3737	0.1435	0.1144	0.3348	0.1422	0.1097
Cumulative	0.3737	0.5173	0.6317	0.3348	0.477	0.5868

Table 5-4.

Navy	1992 Factor 1	1992 Factor 2	1992 Factor 3	1996 Factor 1	1996 Factor 2	1996 Factor 3
I have the skills I need to do my job	0.20798	0.5654	0.42013	0.26698	0.5531	-0.13907
Job makes good use of my skills and abilities	0.57513	0.34702	0.0307	****	****	****
(Organization makes good use of my skills and abilities)	****	****	****	0.59624	0.3964	0.13717
Immediate supervisor has good leadership skills	0.8206	-0.41364	0.19139	****	****	****
(My supervisor has good management skills)	****	****	****	0.64867	-0.26398	-0.27773
Immediate supervisor organized group effectively	0.8104	-0.39173	0.20452	****	****	****
(Supervisor has organized work effectively)	****	****	****	0.86592	0.20067	-0.19963
Overall, I'm satisfied with my supervisor	0.83788	-0.35581	0.13334	0.85995	-0.28287	-0.20233
Cooperation and teamwork exist in unit	0.67645	0.13529	0.13625	****	****	****
(Spirit of cooperation exists in work unit)	****	****	****	0.56319	0.07846	0.30843
Unit customers are satisfied with quality	0.38898	0.42835	0.44892	****	****	****
Awards in unit go to the most deserving	0.66429	0.12069	-4.9900	****	****	****
(My organization promotes on relative ability)	****	****	****	0.47206	0.19188	0.55536
I have been treated fairly in awards	0.5851	0.15541	-0.60567	0.52826	-0.10395	0.55941
I have independence in how I do my work	0.50684	0.41159	-0.23773	****	****	****
(I have more flexibility in the last two years)	****	****	****	0.54177	0.0903	-0.24989
NPR had improved customer service	****	****	****	0.19352	0.66651	0.29742
Eigenvalue	4.0556	1.3012	1.1661	3.7927	1.1592	1.0636
Difference	2.7545	0.135	0.3754	2.6335	0.0956	0.1582
Proportion	0.4056	0.1301	0.1166	0.3793	0.1159	0.1064
Cumulative	0.4056	0.5357	0.6523	0.3793	0.4952	0.6015

Table 5-5.

Office of Personnel Management	1992			1996		
	Factor 1	Factor 2	Factor 3	Factor 1	Factor 2	Factor 3
I have the skills I need to do my job	0.29775	0.53003	0.27365	0.32064	-0.60816	0.30964
Job makes good use of my skills and abilities	0.5267	0.33683	0.04017	****	****	****
(Organization makes good use of my skills and abilities)	****	****	****	0.70365	0.26476	0.2057
Immediate supervisor has good leadership skills	0.81711	-0.43297	0.00666	****	****	****
(My supervisor has good management skills)	****	****	****	0.87212	-0.0278	-0.1867
Immediate supervisor organized group effectively	0.8112	-0.40001	0.07378	****	****	****
(Supervisor has organized work effectively)	****	****	****	0.85785	-0.09709	-0.1732
Overall, I'm satisfied with my supervisor	0.85025	-0.34558	0.04985	0.86177	-0.03985	-0.2546
Cooperation and teamwork exist in unit	0.62639	-0.02518	0.15964	****	****	****
(Spirit of cooperation exists in work unit)	****	****	****	0.65874	-0.17329	-0.18878
Unit customers are satisfied with quality	0.4554	0.28922	0.35905	****	****	****
Awards in unit go to the most deserving	0.62676	0.23291	-0.54356	****	****	****
(My organization promotes on relative ability)	****	****	****	0.44855	-0.13764	0.6533
I have been treated fairly in awards	0.57297	0.37857	-0.56407	0.48656	-0.09907	0.5677
I have independence in how I do my work	0.47815	0.33051	0.39747	****	****	****
(I have more flexibility in the last two years)	****	****	****	0.58806	0.3568	-0.1747
NPR had improved customer service	****	****	****	0.21536	0.76581	0.1480
Eigenvalue	3.9642	1.2524	1.0105	4.1046	1.2243	1.0107
Difference	2.7118	0.2419	0.1681	2.8803	0.2137	0.168
Proportion	0.3964	0.1252	0.101	0.4105	0.1224	0.1011
Cumulative	0.3964	0.5217	0.6227	0.4105	0.5329	0.634

Table 5-6.

Department of Environmental Protection Agency	1992			1996		
	Factor 1	Factor 2	Factor 3	Factor 1	Factor 2	Factor 3
I have the skills I need to do my job	0.18068	0.21878	0.79734	0.21847	0.25952	0.764
Job makes good use of my skills and abilities	0.55629	-0.20260	0.37048	****	****	****
(Organization makes good use of my skills and abilities)	****	****	****	****	0.30722	0.26236
Immediate supervisor has good leadership skills	0.84184	0.0407	-0.22058	****	****	****
(My supervisor has good management skills)	****	****	****	****	-0.35154	0.09398
Immediate supervisor organized group effectively	0.82333	0.19272	-0.24045	****	****	****
(Supervisor has organized work effectively)	****	****	****	0.81434	-0.30518	0.0592
Overall, I'm satisfied with my supervisor	0.84656	-0.01901	-0.19346	0.82035	-0.37431	0.0981
Cooperation and teamwork exist in unit	0.65607	0.32823	-0.03152	****	****	****
(Spirit of cooperation exists in work unit)	****	****	****	0.63748	0.02776	-0.14318
Unit customers are satisfied with quality	0.35822	0.68883	0.20388	****	****	****
Awards in unit go to the most deserving	0.66241	-0.18708	-0.00455	****	****	****
(My organization promotes on relative ability)	****	****	****	0.43997	0.48039	-0.2465
I have been treated fairly in awards	0.59006	-0.44074	0.00289	0.46557	0.40303	-0.2321
I have independence in how I do my work	0.38707	-0.46960	0.37779	****	****	****
(I have more flexibility in the last two years)	****	****	****	0.55122	0.18436	-0.4296
NPR had improved customer service	****	****	****	0.17568	0.64392	-.1612
Eigenvalue	3.9409	1.1601	1.1022	3.5412	1.3611	1.0203
Difference	2.7808	0.0578	0.1765	2.1801	0.3409	0.0987
Proportion	0.3941	0.116	0.1102	0.3541	0.1361	0.102
Cumulative	0.3941	0.5101	0.6203	0.3541	0.4902	0.5923

Table 5-7.

Department of Housing and Urban Development	1992 Factor 1	1992 Factor 2	1992 Factor 3	1996 Factor 1	1996 Factor 2	1996 Factor 3
I have the skills I need to do my job	0.05495	0.75779	0.31503	2.8499	0.28356	0.40649
Job makes good use of my skills and abilities	0.57485	0.20564	-0.0881	****	****	-0.11053
(Organization makes good use of my skills and abilities)	****	****	0.27017	0.63545	0.47948	****
Immediate supervisor has good leadership skills	0.84906	-0.27977	****	****	****	0.0297
(My supervisor has good management skills)	****	****	0.34586	0.85192	-0.40936	****
Immediate supervisor organized group effectively	0.79595	-0.27264	****	****	****	-0.0293
(Supervisor has organized work effectively)	****	****	0.17555	0.83198	-0.42227	-0.00027
Overall, I'm satisfied with my supervisor	0.85838	-0.21524	0.14032	0.81849	-0.46171	****
Cooperation and teamwork exist in unit	0.66427	0.04077	****	****	****	-0.2730
(Spirit of cooperation exists in work unit)	****	****	0.19751	0.53443	0.2118	****
Unit customers are satisfied with quality	0.478	0.51518	-0.44155	****	****	****
Awards in unit go to the most deserving	0.70029	0.10919	****	****	****	0.38305
(My organization promotes on relative ability)	****	****	-0.61361	0.47989	0.20468	0.6429
I have been treated fairly in awards	0.62412	0.06319	-0.20863	0.31746	0.29838	-0.2068
I have independence in how I do my work	0.56308	0.16022	****	****	****	****
(I have more flexibility in the last two years)	****	****	****	0.56003	0.33808	-0.4321
NPR had improved customer service	****	****	****	0.40677	0.48429	****
Eigenvalue	4.2914	1.1241	1.0042	3.6687	1.394	1.036
Difference	3.1673	0.12	0.1136	2.2747	0.358	0.1146
Proportion	0.4291	0.1124	0.1004	0.3669	0.1394	0.1036
Cumulative	0.4291	0.5416	0.642	0.3669	0.5063	0.6099

customers satisfied" of .45 and a negative loading of -.63 of "I have been treated fairly in awards." In the Department of State (Table 5-8) the third dimension contains a positive loading of .53 for "Unit customers are satisfied with quality," and a negative loadings for "Awards in unit go to the most deserving" (-.45) and "I have been fairly treated on awards" (-.55). For the Department of Transportation (Table 5-9) the second dimension contains a positive loading of .58 for "Unit customers are satisfied with quality," and a negative loading for "I have been treated fairly on awards" (-.41). Finally for the SBA (Table 5-2) these questions load at .69 and -.47 respectively.

In summary these inverse relationships may imply that employees (in the six agencies) do not see the system of awards supporting the concept of "customer satisfaction" in 1992. In view of these trends this book posits the following question: how has the NPR changed the merit reward structure of the federal agencies so that "attention to the customer" is rewarded?

Changes in the Factor Pattern Structure - 1992 to 1996

An in-depth examination of the factor pattern structure for 1996 reveals a change in the factor patterns for the following cultural questions: "I have the skills I need to do my job," "Awards go to most deserving," "I have been treated fairly in awards," and "Unit customers are satisfied with quality." These changes occurred in the Departments of Commerce, Navy, Agriculture, Labor, Transportation, Energy and Housing and Urban Development, OPM and the Small Business Administration.

The Relationship Of Customer Service To Awards

Within the Departments of State, Treasury, Housing and Urban Development and the Small Business Administration the loadings for the customer service question were inversely related to the merit "award" questions in 1992. In 1996, after four years of NPR implementation, customer service remained inversely related to the perception of fairness in awards within these agencies. For the Department of Housing and Urban Development and the Small Business Administration these questions had stronger inverse relationships than in 1992.

In 1992 dimension three within the State Department (Table 5-8)

Table 5-8.

State Department

	1992			1996		
	Factor 1	Factor 2	Factor 3	Factor 1	Factor 2	Factor 3
I have the skills I need to do my job	0.23052	0.43966	0.5648	0.31751	-0.42218	-0.15331
Job makes good use of my skills and abilities	0.52411	0.50222	-0.0411	****	****	****
(Organization makes good use of my skills and abilities)	****	****	****	0.64688	0.32682	0.0410
Immediate supervisor has good leadership skills	0.83253	-0.43186	0.01222	****	****	0.1027
(My supervisor has good management skills)	****	****	****	0.85487	-0.21716	****
Immediate supervisor organized group effectively	0.83763	-0.4146	0.02628	****	****	****
(Supervisor has organized work effectively)	****	****	****	0.83877	-0.15066	0.0710
Overall, I'm satisfied with my supervisor	0.83411	-0.42612	0.01064	0.87427	-0.19167	0.0655
Cooperation and teamwork exist in unit	0.64143	0.20738	0.08953	****	****	****
(Spirit of cooperation exists in work unit)	****	****	****	0.58892	-0.27602	-0.1726
Unit customers are satisfied with quality	0.37122	0.10272	0.52837	****	****	****
Awards in unit go to the most deserving	0.60008	0.37037	-0.4529	****	****	****
(My organization promotes on relative ability)	****	****	****	0.47259	0.43356	-0.4644
I have been treated fairly in awards	0.46302	0.3909	-0.55323	0.3947	0.60626	-0.3633
I have independence in how I do my work	0.38404	0.32101	0.32456	****	****	****
(I have more flexibility in the last two years)	****	****	****	0.48818	0.12528	-0.3459
NPR had improved customer service	****	****	****	0.14497	0.40994	-0.7303
Eigenvalue	3.6895	1.321	1.2253	3.7032	1.2071	1.0769
Difference	2.2574	0.2067	0.3774	2.4961	0.1302	0.1621
Proportion	0.369	0.1432	0.1225	0.3703	0.1207	0.1077
Cumulative	0.369	0.5122	0.6347	0.3703	0.491	0.5987

Table 5-9.

Transportation Department	1992			1996		
	Factor 1	Factor 2	Factor 3	Factor 1	Factor 2	Factor 3
I have the skills I need to do my job	0.08917	0.72127	0.11194	0.25592	0.35502	****
Job makes good use of my skills and abilities	0.51228	0.23519	0.20569	****	****	****
(Organization makes good use of my skills and abilities)	****	****	****	0.66326	0.3212	****
Immediate supervisor has good leadership skills	0.83504	-0.11323	-0.40033	****	****	****
(My supervisor has good management skills)	****	****	****	0.85792	-0.37562	****
Immediate supervisor organized group effectively	0.81472	-0.0564	-0.39323	****	****	****
(Supervisor has organized work effectively)	****	****	****	0.83721	-0.35887	****
Overall, I'm satisfied with my supervisor	0.85837	-0.13041	-0.31734	0.84164	-0.3956	****
Cooperation and teamwork exist in unit	0.69238	0.24791	0.0601	****	****	****
(Spirit of cooperation exists in work unit)	****	****	****	0.55145	0.19629	****
Unit customers are satisfied with quality	0.34304	0.57522	0.17756	****	****	****
Awards in unit go to the most deserving	0.59522	-0.31821	0.52097	****	****	****
(My organization promotes on relative ability)	****	****	****	0.48094	0.34022	****
I have been treated fairly in awards	0.51672	-0.40631	0.56846	0.41596	0.28012	****
I have independence in how I do my work	0.49757	0.19701	0.21172	****	****	****
(I have more flexibility in the last two years)	****	****	****	0.57448	0.26037	****
NPR had improved customer service	****	****	****	0.19878	0.57243	****
Eigenvalue	3.8342	1.306	1.145	3.7287	1.2838	****
Difference	2.5281	0.1611	0.3351	2.4449	0.3466	****
Proportion	0.3834	0.1306	0.1145	0.3729	0.1284	****
Cumulative	0.3834	0.514	0.6285	0.3729	0.5012	****

Table 5-10.

U.S. Department of Agriculture	1992 Factor 1	1992 Factor 2	1992 Factor 3	1996 Factor 1	1996 Factor 2	1996 Factor 3
I have the skills I need to do my job	0.25221	0.78755	****	0.26655	0.12672	****
Job makes good use of my skills and abilities	0.57824	0.3469	****	****	****	****
(Organization makes good use of my skills and abilities)	****	****	****	0.66783	0.23119	****
Immediate supervisor has good leadership skills	0.85925	-0.20532	****	****	****	****
(My supervisor has good management skills)	****	****	****	0.86871	-0.3203	****
Immediate supervisor organized group effectively	0.83028	-0.18574	****	****	****	****
(Supervisor has organized work effectively)	****	****	****	0.86123	-0.28648	****
Overall, I'm satisfied with my supervisor	0.85737	-0.22255	****	0.8474	-0.38595	****
Cooperation and teamwork exist in unit	0.70175	0.03405	****	****	****	****
(Spirit of cooperation exists in work unit)	****	****	****	0.58843	0.11978	****
Unit customers are satisfied with quality	0.48108	0.32026	****	****	****	****
Awards in unit go to the most deserving	0.60772	-0.0993	****	****	****	****
(My organization promotes on relative ability)	****	****	****	0.45856	0.40019	****
I have been treated fairly in awards	0.56985	-0.17896	****	0.42234	0.48342	****
I have independence in how I do my work	0.49971	0.2133	****	****	****	****
(I have more flexibility in the last two years)	****	****	****	0.58472	0.13221	****
NPR had improved customer service	****	****	****	0.23417	0.54826	****
Eigenvalue	4.2284	1.0579	****	3.8631	1.1294	****
Difference	3.1705	0.0854	****	2.7337	0.1405	****
Proportion	0.4228	0.1058	****	0.3863	0.1129	****
Cumulative	0.4288	0.5286	****	0.3863	0.4993	****

contained a positive loading of .53 for "Unit customers satisfied with quality," and a negative loading of -.55 for "I have been treated fairly on awards." In 1996 these questions continued to load inversely (.73 and -.46 in dimension three). Likewise, in the Department of Housing and Urban Development, (Table 5-7) a stronger inverse relationship emerged on these questions. For HUD, in 1992 dimension three contains a positive loading of .20 for "Unit customers satisfied with quality," while "I have been treated fairly in awards" has a negative loading of -.61. In 1996, "I have been treated fairly in awards" has a positive loading of .64, while "NPR had improved customer service" has a negative loading of -.42.

For Treasury in 1992, dimension three contained a positive loading for "unit customers satisfied" of .45, and a negative loading of -.63 for "I have been treated fairly on awards." In 1996, the relationship between these cultural questions remained inverse. "NPR had improved customer service" loaded at .31, and "I have been treated fairly on awards" had a negative loading of -.41. For the Small Business Administration in 1996, dimension three contained negative loadings of -.43 for "NPR had improved customer service" and -.25 for "I have been treated fairly in awards." In contrast in 1992, these questions loaded .69 and -.47 respectively.

In contrast to the above four federal agencies (where customer service was found to be inverse to awards), the relationship of the customer service question to "merit awards" became more direct and positive in the Department of Navy and the Department of Agriculture during the study time period. In 1996 within the Department of Navy (Table 5-4) "NPR had improved customer service" loaded at .30, while "I have been treated fairly on awards" loaded at .56. In 1992 the relationship between these two questions were inverse; "I have been treated fairly on awards" had a negative loading of -.61, while "unit customer are satisfied with quality" had a positive loading of .45. Like the Navy, the Department of Agriculture (Table 5-10) shows a more positive and direct relationship between customer service and awards in 1996. For example, in 1992 the question "Unit customers satisfied with quality" had a positive loading of .32, and a negative loading of -.18 for "I have been treated fairly in awards." In 1996 the second dimension for Agriculture contained positive loadings of .55 for "NPR had improved customer service" and .48 for "I have been treated fairly in awards."

The Relationship of Customer Service To Employee Skills

An examination of the factor pattern structure for the questions "Unit customers satisfied with quality" and "I have the skills needed to do my job" reveals that an inverse relationship developed between these questions during the study time period. This change in the factor pattern structure occurred in the Departments of Labor and Commerce, the Office of Personnel Management and the Small Business Administration. For the Commerce Department (Table 5-11) dimension three in 1996 contains a positive loading of .82 for the question "I have the skills needed to do my job," and a negative loading of -.58 for "NPR had improved customer service." In the Labor Department (Table 5-12) factor three contains a positive loading of .89 for the employee skills question, and a negative loading of -.37 for the NPR question. In 1996 within OPM (Table 5-5) employee skills is inversely related to the NPR question. Dimension two contains a positive loading of .76 for "NPR had improved customer service," and a negative loading of -.61 for "I have the skills I need to do my job." Finally for the Small Business Administration dimension three shows an inverse relationship between these questions. In 1996 for SBA "I have the skills to do my job" loads positively at .81, while "NPR had improved customer service" has a negative loading of -.43. The patterns that emerged in these agencies imply that as employees see that they have "less skills" they may view this change as a function of the National Performance Review.

The Relationship Of Merit Awards To Employee Skills

For the Departments of Transportation, Housing and Urban Development and Energy a different pattern emerges on the relationship of the merit awards question to employee skills. For example, in DOT (Table 5-19) there is an inverse relationship between "I have been treated fairly on awards" (-.41) and "I have the skills I need to do my job" (.72) for dimension two in 1992. In 1996 the relationship between these two questions is more positive and direct, but not at a level of significance (. 28 and .36). In the Department of Energy, (Table 5-16) the second dimension in 1996 contains a positive loading of .69 for the cultural question "I have skills I need to do my job," and a positive loading of .42 for "I have been treated fairly in awards." In 1992 the correlations between these questions were not as strong (.67 and .17).

Likewise, for the Department of Housing and Urban Development in 1996 the third dimensions contain a positive loading of .64 for "I have been treated fairly in awards," and a positive loading of .41 for "I have the skills I need in my job." In 1992 these questions loaded inversely (-.62 and .31).

In contrast to the changes noted in the factor pattern structure for these three agencies no discernable change was observed in the Treasury Department and NASA. For Treasury, the merit award question remained inversely related to the question on employee skills; in 1992 "I have the skills I need to do my job" in dimension three contained a positive loading of .44, while "Awards go to deserving" loaded negatively at -.54. In 1996 these questions continue to load inversely (.76 and -.48). Likewise for NASA (Table 5-21) the "skills" and "awards" questions loaded inversely to each other in 1992 (.48 and -.49 within dimensions 2). In 1996 the relationship between these questions remains inverse, albeit not at a level of significance (.74 and -.15).

Table 5-11.

U.S. Department of Commerce

	1992			1996		
	Factor 1	Factor 2	Factor 3	Factor 1	Factor 2	Factor 3
I have the skills I need to do my job	0.23558	0.57236	0.33162	0.19373	0.22154	0.81914
Job makes good use of my skills and abilities	0.58555	0.26821	0.01108	****	****	****
(Organization makes good use of my skills and abilities)	****	****	****	0.65453	0.37012	0.04561
Immediate supervisor has good leadership skills	0.82001	-0.43611	0.1655	****	****	****
(My supervisor has good management skills)	****	****	****	0.86427	-0.29772	-0.09447
Immediate supervisor organized group effectively	0.82	-0.36169	0.22072	****	****	****
(Supervisor has organized work effectively)	****	****	****	0.85853	-0.11477	-0.06435
Overall, I'm satisfied with my supervisor	0.85449	-0.3502	0.112551	0.88862	-0.27333	-0.05163
Cooperation and teamwork exist in unit	0.62626	0.13555	0.11595	****	****	****
(Spirit of cooperation exists in work unit)	****	****	****	0.59911	-0.08145	0.06744
Unit customers are satisfied with quality	0.37397	0.50227	0.43156	****	****	****
Awards in unit go to the most deserving	0.66095	0.06171	-0.55782	****	****	****
(My organization promotes on relative ability)	****	****	****	0.50946	0.16115	0.02265
I have been treated fairly in awards	0.51677	0.27849	-0.6684	0.13508	0.37429	-0.08599
I have independence in how I do my work	0.51669	0.3958	-0.03359	****	****	****
(I have more flexibility in the last two years)	****	****	****	0.4485	0.5505	0.13272
NPR had improved customer service	****	****	****	0.15341	0.52015	-0.57644
Eigenvalue	3.9763	1.3513	1.1576	3.6951	1.1944	1.0512
Difference	2.6250	0.1937	0.3106	2.5007	0.1433	0.0816
Proportion	0.3976	0.1351	0.1158	0.3695	0.1194	0.1051
Cumulative	0.3976	0.5328	0.6485	0.3695	0.4889	0.5941

Table 5-12.

Labor Department	1992			1996		
	Factor 1	Factor 2	Factor 3	Factor 1	Factor 2	Factor 3
I have the skills I need to do my job	0.27657	0.44676	0.57297	0.15226	-0.04071	0.89213
Job makes good use of my skills and abilities	0.55105	0.35542	-0.15363	****	****	****
(Organization makes good use of my skills and abilities)	****	****	****	****	0.27099	0.19793
Immediate supervisor has good leadership skills	0.82822	-0.39698	0.23716	****	****	****
(My supervisor has good management skills)	****	****	****	****	-0.30973	****
Immediate supervisor organized group effectively	0.83968	-0.32119	0.24842	****	****	****
(Supervisor has organized work effectively)	****	****	****	0.85786	-0.30191	-0.13618
Overall, I'm satisfied with my supervisor	0.86067	-0.34277	0.17145	0.8755	-0.29058	****
Cooperation and teamwork exist in unit	0.65607	0.14446	-0.05894	****	****	****
(Spirit of cooperation exists in work unit)	****	****	****	0.53081	-0.05475	****
Unit customers are satisfied with quality	0.37098	0.60775	0.20424	****	****	****
Awards in unit go to the most deserving	0.6876	0.10265	-0.45373	****	****	****
(My organization promotes on relative ability)	****	****	****	0.36188	0.50682	0.03986
I have been treated fairly in awards	0.6205	0.01693	-0.49849	0.39381	0.42145	0.10846
I have independence in how I do my work	0.49905	0.34618	-0.08454	****	****	****
(I have more flexibility in the last two years)	****	****	****	0.47872	0.35938	****
NPR had improved customer service	****	****	****	0.19819	0.63007	****
Eigenvalue	4.1868	1.2251	1.0059	3.5148	1.3102	1.0846
Difference	2.9618	0.2191	0.1618	2.2046	0.2256	0.2012
Proportion	0.4187	0.1225	0.1006	0.3515	0.131	0.1085
Cumulative	0.4187	0.5412	0.6418	0.3515	0.4825	0.591

Table 5-13.

Air Force	1992			1996		
	Factor 1	Factor 2	Factor 3	Factor 1	Factor 2	Factor 3
I have the skills I need to do my job	0.32938	0.04287	0.66219	0.12394	0.17161	0.61401
Job makes good use of my skills and abilities	0.61167	0.22944	0.28784	****	****	****
(Organization makes good use of my skills and abilities)	****	****	****	0.67764	0.3827	-0.1662
Immediate supervisor has good leadership skills	0.83012	-0.31459	-0.30274	****	****	****
(My supervisor has good management skills)	****	****	****	0.8573	0.41762	0.02601
Immediate supervisor organised group effectively	0.80761	-0.38081	-0.18791	****	****	****
(Supervisor has organized work effectively)	****	****	****	0.84022	-0.3916	0.03097
Overall, I'm satisfied with my supervisor	0.83512	-0.29244	-0.26384	0.84223	0.43423	0.05351
Cooperation and teamwork exist in unit	0.60513	-0.01398	0.24342	****	****	****
(Spirit of cooperation exists in work unit)	****	****	****	0.60289	0.27428	-0.24744
Unit customers are satisfied with quality	0.44223	-0.14303	0.51182	****	****	****
Awards in unit go to the most deserving	0.5693	0.58321	-0.20659	****	****	****
(My organization promotes on relative ability)	****	****	****	0.4649	0.48983	-0.22029
I have been treated fairly in awards	0.47779	0.65151	-0.25653	0.51899	0.33849	0.01678
I have independence in how I do my work	0.50189	0.17337	0.152	****	****	****
(I have more flexibility in the last two years)	****	****	****	0.58877	0.28986	0.1184
NPR had improved customer service	****	****	****	0.16485	0.19877	0.70551
Eigenvalue	3.9907	1.2019	1.1707	3.8476	1.2455	1.0309
Difference	2.7888	0.0312	0.3664	2.6021	0.2146	0.0533
Proportion	0.3991	0.1202	0.1171	0.3848	0.1246	0.1031
Cumulative	0.3991	0.5193	0.6363	0.3848	0.5093	0.6124

Table 5-14.

Army	1992			1996		
	Factor 1	Factor 2	Factor 3	Factor 1	Factor 2	Factor 3
I have the skills I need to do my job	0.09521	0.72134	****	0.39669	0.12351	****
Job makes good use of my skills and abilities	0.60782	0.30013	****	****	****	****
(Organization makes good use of my skills and abilities)	****	****	****	0.6589	0.30519	****
Immediate supervisor has good leadership skills	0.84705	-0.27734	****	****	****	****
(My supervisor has good management skills)	****	****	****	0.85738	0.36582	****
Immediate supervisor organized group effectively	0.83634	-0.24605	****	****	****	****
(Supervisor has organized work effectively)	****	****	****	0.8561	-0.34489	****
Overall, I'm satisfied with my supervisor	0.84715	-0.27758	****	0.8713	-0.31674	****
Cooperation and teamwork exist in unit	0.66125	0.10401	****	****	****	****
(Spirit of cooperation exists in work unit)	****	****	****	0.62318	0.09949	****
Unit customers are satisfied with quality	0.38274	0.55393	****	****	****	****
Awards in unit go to the most deserving	0.68149	0.04194	****	****	****	****
(My organization promotes on relative ability)	****	****	****	0.32933	0.49001	****
I have been treated fairly in awards	0.58452	0.05034	****	0.43664	0.33236	****
I have independence in how I do my work	0.48476	0.1773	****	****	****	****
(I have more flexibility in the last two years)	****	****	****	0.48982	0.33792	****
NPR had improved customer service	****	****	****	0.20808	0.48217	****
Eigenvalue	4.138	1.1783	****	3.7867	1.1686	****
Difference	2.9597	0.1786	****	2.618	0.1115	****
Proportion	0.4138	0.1178	****	0.3787	0.1169	****
Cumulative	0.4138	0.5316	****	0.3787	0.4955	****

Table 5-15.

Department of Education	1992			1996		
	Factor 1	Factor 2	Factor 3	Factor 1	Factor 2	Factor 3
I have the skills I need to do my job	0.16868	0.81085	****	0.0646	0.32343	****
Job makes good use of my skills and abilities	0.67207	0.14865	****	****	****	****
(Organization makes good use of my skills and abilities)	****	****	****	0.74057	0.16995	****
Immediate supervisor has good leadership skills	0.85459	-0.16552	****	****	****	****
(My supervisor has good management skills)	****	****	****	0.83804	-0.38327	****
Immediate supervisor organized group effectively	0.85578	-0.18334	****	****	****	****
(Supervisor has organized work effectively)	****	****	****	0.86941	-0.2692	****
Overall, I'm satisfied with my supervisor	0.8568	-0.20589	****	0.84271	-0.37515	****
Cooperation and teamwork exist in unit	0.73292	-0.25638	****	****	****	****
(Spirit of cooperation exists in work unit)	****	****	****	0.589	0.31252	****
Unit customers are satisfied with quality	0.5723	0.09948	****	****	****	****
Awards in unit go to the most deserving	0.68973	0.16365	****	****	****	****
(My organization promotes on relative ability)	****	****	****	0.43621	0.29336	****
I have been treated fairly in awards	0.56999	0.39589	****	0.45349	-0.03162	****
I have independence in how I do my work	0.6332	0.04821	****	****	****	****
(I have more flexibility in the last two years)	****	****	****	0.5788	0.37262	****
NPR had improved customer service	****	****	****	0.33447	0.63162	****
Eigenvalue	4.7432	1.0444	****	3.9107	1.2161	****
Difference	3.6988	0.0962	****	2.6946	0.2047	****
Proportion	0.4743	0.1044	****	0.3911	0.1216	****
Cumulative	0.4743	0.5788	****	0.3911	0.5127	****

Table 5-16.

Department of Energy	1992 Factor 1	1992 Factor 2	1992 Factor 3	1996 Factor 1	1996 Factor 2	1996 Factor 3
I have the skills I need to do my job	0.20501	0.66771	****	0.11032	0.68866	****
Job makes good use of my skills and abilities	0.62194	0.27417	****	****	****	****
(Organization makes good use of my skills and abilities)	****	****	****	0.70024	0.26035	****
Immediate supervisor has good leadership skills	0.82726	-0.40404	****	****	****	****
(My supervisor has good management skills)	****	****	****	0.85903	-0.28731	****
Immediate supervisor organized group effectively	0.82946	-0.31072	****	****	****	****
(Supervisor has organized work effectively)	****	****	****	0.83639	-0.28755	****
Overall, I'm satisfied with my supervisor	0.84029	-0.35248	****	0.86446	-0.24111	****
Cooperation and teamwork exist in unit	0.66411	0.06942	****	****	****	****
(Spirit of cooperation exists in work unit)	****	****	****	0.59867	-0.06882	****
Unit customers are satisfied with quality	0.35051	0.50087	****	0.52799	0.36568	****
Awards in unit go to the most deserving	0.63414	0.21251	****	****	****	****
(My organization promotes on relative ability)	****	****	****	0.45941	0.4207	****
I have been treated fairly in awards	0.5993	0.17163	****	****	****	****
I have independence in how I do my work	0.56837	0.20278	****	****	****	****
(I have more flexibility in the last two years)	****	****	****	0.56128	0.15625	****
NPR had improved customer service	****	****	****	0.11728	0.03933	****
Eigenvalue	4.1555	1.2821	****	3.8643	1.1068	****
Difference	2.8734	0.3012	****	2.7575	0.0289	****
Proportion	0.4156	0.1282	****	0.3864	0.1107	****
Cumulative	0.4156	0.5438	****	0.3864	0.4971	****

Table 5-17.

General Services Administration	1992 Factor 1	1992 Factor 2	1992 Factor 3	1996 Factor 1	1996 Factor 2	1996 Factor 3
I have the skills I need to do my job	0.34331	0.56813	0.07537	0.22143	0.44638	0.18841
Job makes good use of my skills and abilities	0.55799	0.19591	0.17023	0.66479	0.32519	****
(Organization makes good use of my skills and abilities)	****	-0.26822	-0.3738	****	****	****
Immediate supervisor has good leadership skills	****	****	****	0.83011	-0.41695	****
(My supervisor has good management skills)	****	-0.16262	-0.38361	****	****	****
Immediate supervisor organized group effectively	****	****	****	0.85649	-0.32876	****
(Supervisor has organized work effectively)	0.86787	-0.20581	0.2854	0.85313	-0.38635	****
Overall, I'm satisfied with my supervisor	0.71641	0.29447	-0.08523	****	****	****
Cooperation and teamwork exist in unit	****	****	****	0.62976	0.17981	-0.21908
(Spirit of cooperation exists in work unit)	0.48905	0.55009	0.02919	****	****	****
Unit customers are satisfied with quality	0.63902	-0.29967	0.48391	****	****	****
Awards in unit go to the most deserving	****	****	****	0.44369	0.23361	****
(My organization promotes on relative ability)	0.55356	-0.38683	0.59454	0.46855	0.22873	****
I have been treated fairly in awards	0.53605	0.28952	0.29873	****	****	****
I have independence in how I do my work	****	****	****	0.58561	0.30579	****
(I have more flexibility in the last two years)	****	****	****	0.24882	0.55915	****
NPR had improved customer service	****	****	****	****	****	****
Eigenvalue	4.2982	1.2145	1.088	3.8593	1.2816	1.0602
Difference	3.0837	0.1265	0.2444	2.5777	0.2214	0.1386
Proportion	0.4298	0.1214	0.1088	0.3859	0.1282	0.106
Cumulative	0.4298	0.5513	0.6601	0.3859	0.5141	0.6201

Table 5-18.

Department of Health and Human Services	1992			1996		
	Factor 1	Factor 2	Factor 3	Factor 1	Factor 2	Factor 3
I have the skills I need to do my job	0.21056	0.63041	****	0.24389	0.40514	****
Job makes good use of my skills and abilities	0.54864	0.14525	****	****	****	****
(Organization makes good use of my skills and abilities)	****	****	****	0.68828	0.37366	****
Immediate supervisor has good leadership skills	0.83715	-0.38899	****	****	****	****
(My supervisor has good management skills)	****	****	****	0.8666	-0.31336	****
Immediate supervisor organized group effectively	0.81565	-0.32435	****	****	****	****
(Supervisor has organized work effectively)	****	****	****	0.87215	-0.25445	****
Overall, I'm satisfied with my supervisor	0.8368	-0.37978	****	0.85878	-0.33609	****
Cooperation and teamwork exist in unit	0.71074	0.10895	****	****	****	****
(Spirit of cooperation exists in work unit)	****	****	****	0.60845	0.07224	****
Unit customers are satisfied with quality	0.38184	0.39069	****	****	****	****
Awards in unit go to the most deserving	0.58699	0.22298	****	0.47376	0.26966	****
(My organization promotes on relative ability)	****	****	****	0.41877	-0.07679	****
I have been treated fairly in awards	0.48984	0.25471	****	****	****	****
I have independence in how I do my work	0.51296	0.41581	****	0.48727	****	****
(I have more flexibility in the last two years)	****	****	****	****	0.41529	****
NPR had improved customer service	****	****	****	0.12959	0.64974	****
Eigenvalue	3.9103	1.2713	****	3.8066	1.2581	****
Difference	2.639	0.1436	****	2.5485	0.2807	****
Proportion	0.391	0.1271	****	0.3807	0.1258	****
Cumulative	0.391	0.5182	****	0.3807	0.5065	****

Table 5-19.

Department of the Interior	1992			1996		
	Factor 1	Factor 2	Factor 3	Factor 1	Factor 2	Factor 3
I have the skills I need to do my job	0.22943	0.5878	****	0.1505	0.43041	****
Job makes good use of my skills and abilities	0.57372	0.33502	****	****	****	****
(Organization makes good use of my skills and abilities)	****	****	****	0.64258	0.35407	****
Immediate supervisor has good leadership skills	0.81161	-0.41865	****	****	****	****
(My supervisor has good management skills)	****	****	****	0.88332	-0.29643	****
Immediate supervisor organized group effectively	0.79944	-0.3856	****	****	****	****
(Supervisor has organized work effectively)	****	****	****	0.86902	-0.30585	****
Overall, I'm satisfied with my supervisor	0.82323	-0.34318	****	0.87936	-0.29666	****
Cooperation and teamwork exist in unit	0.6569	0.0758	****	****	****	****
(Spirit of cooperation exists in work unit)	****	****	****	0.63543	-0.00476	****
Unit customers are satisfied with quality	0.44358	0.44454	****	****	****	****
Awards in unit go to the most deserving	0.60115	0.16239	****	****	****	****
(My organization promotes on relative ability)	****	****	****	0.46595	0.33874	****
I have been treated fairly in awards	0.50928	0.11512	****	0.46647	0.26329	****
I have independence in how I do my work	0.58392	0.34786	****	****	****	****
(I have more flexibility in the last two years)	****	****	****	0.52879	****	****
NPR had improved customer service	****	****	****	0.20028	****	****
Eigenvalue	3.9572	1.2642	****	3.9025	1.2492	****
Difference	2.693	0.1595	****	2.6533	0.2662	****
Proportion	0.3957	0.1264	****	0.3902	0.1249	****
Cumulative	0.3957	0.5221	****	0.3902	0.5152	****

Table 5-20.

Justice Department	1992			1996		
	Factor 1	Factor 2	Factor 3	Factor 1	Factor 2	Factor 3
I have the skills I need to do my job	0.08717	0.38994	0.70256	0.19204	0.15371	0.87945
Job makes good use of my skills and abilities	0.61109	0.25944	0.248	****	0.39732	0.10296
(Organization makes good use of my skills and abilities)	****	****	****	****	****	****
Immediate supervisor has good leadership skills	0.80209	-0.47695	0.01302	****	****	****
(My supervisor has good management skills)	****	****	****	****	-0.28943	0.00268
Immediate supervisor organized group effectively	0.84532	-0.39592	0.01679	****	****	****
(Supervisor has organized work effectively)	****	****	****	0.87236	-0.27902	****
Overall, I'm satisfied with my supervisor	0.83959	-0.40218	****	0.86761	-0.33037	****
Cooperation and teamwork exist in unit	0.73708	0.00748	****	****	****	****
(Spirit of cooperation exists in work unit)	****	****	****	0.61304	-0.04134	0.03227
Unit customers are satisfied with quality	0.52538	0.24732	0.37002	****	****	****
Awards in unit go to the most deserving	0.63487	0.39661	-0.37903	****	****	****
(My organization promotes on relative ability)	****	****	****	0.49108	0.38573	****
I have been treated fairly in awards	0.57435	0.43846	-0.46567	0.47051	0.17505	****
I have independence in how I do my work	0.53779	.41523	-0.11566	****	****	****
(I have more flexibility in the last two years)	****	****	****	0.59349	0.25303	****
NPR had improved customer service	****	****	****	0.15447	0.71568	****
Eigenvalue	4.2853	1.3485	1.088	3.9064	1.2096	1.0256
Difference	2.9368	0.2605	0.2542	2.6968	0.184	0.1616
Proportion	0.4285	0.1349	0.1088	0.3906	0.121	0.1026
Cumulative	0.4258	0.5634	0.6722	0.3906	0.5116	0.6142

Table 5-21.

NASA	1992 Factor 1	1992 Factor 2	1992 Factor 3	1996 Factor 1	1996 Factor 2	1996 Factor 3
I have the skills I need to do my job	0.21557	0.63564	0.47887	0.20163	-0.12051	0.74346
Job makes good use of my skills and abilities	0.615	0.40053	0.0613	****	0.1493	****
(Organization makes good use of my skills and abilities)	****	****	****	0.6758	****	****
Immediate supervisor has good leadership skills	0.81285	-0.39778	0.20759	****	****	****
(My supervisor has good management skills)	****	****	****	0.87494	-0.31205	****
Immediate supervisor organized group effectively	0.77061	-0.41482	0.24658	****	****	****
(Supervisor has organized work effectively)	****	****	****	0.85811	-0.34439	****
Overall, I'm satisfied with my supervisor	0.85402	-0.3148	0.19155	0.88479	-0.29594	****
Cooperation and teamwork exist in unit	0.70376	0.15257	-0.01894	****	****	****
(Spirit of cooperation exists in work unit)	****	****	****	0.55344	0.29178	-0.6196
Unit customers are satisfied with quality	0.50972	0.29767	0.04942	****	****	****
Awards in unit go to the most deserving	0.7107	0.0135	-0.48553	****	****	****
(My organization promotes on relative ability)	****	****	****	0.45797	0.51725	****
I have been treated fairly in awards	0.55942	0.15775	-0.62887	0.42999	0.63728	****
I have independence in how I do my work	0.60577	0.28818	0.03587	****	****	****
(I have more flexibility in the last two years)	****	****	****	0.413	0.13416	****
NPR had improved customer service	****	****	****	0.2256	0.11518	****
Eigenvalue	4.3487	1.211	1.009	3.7045	1.1304	1.0271
Difference	3.1377	0.202	0.1905	2.574	0.1034	0.077
Proportion	0.4349	0.1211	0.1009	0.3704	0.113	0.1027
Cumulative	0.4349	0.556	0.6569	0.3704	0.4835	0.5862

Table 5-22.

Veteran Affairs	1992			1996		
	Factor 1	Factor 2	Factor 3	Factor 1	Factor 2	Factor 3
I have the skills I need to do my job	0.24494	0.46865	-0.29802	0.23532	-0.40506	0.61934
Job makes good use of my skills and abilities	0.58629	0.41493	-0.07181	0.66232	0.10374	0.32686
(Organization makes good use of my skills and abilities)	****	****	****	****	****	****
Immediate supervisor has good leadership skills	0.82256	-0.3985	-0.23116	0.8633	-0.15801	-0.21901
(My supervisor has good management skills)	****	****	****	****	****	****
Immediate supervisor organized group effectively	0.79323	-0.36159	-0.28347	0.87002	-0.21141	-0.11858
(Supervisor has organized work effectively)	****	****	****	****	****	****
Overall, I'm satisfied with my supervisor	0.82499	-0.36662	-0.19752	0.87099	-0.18965	-0.18772
Cooperation and teamwork exist in unit	0.69512	0.29026	-0.00626	0.56975	-0.05348	0.09888
(Spirit of cooperation exists in work unit)	****	****	****	****	****	****
Unit customers are satisfied with quality	0.45188	0.49679	-0.23762	0.39762	0.63709	-0.14196
Awards in unit go to the most deserving	0.60439	-0.00217	0.57953	0.44109	0.31717	-0.34609
(My organization promotes on relative ability)	****	****	****	****	****	****
I have been treated fairly in awards	0.51256	-0.12222	0.66744	0.61202	0.08484	0.27457
I have independence in how I do my work	0.4867	0.43806	0.23098	****	****	****
(I have more flexibility in the last two years)	****	****	****	****	****	****
NPR had improved customer service	****	****	****	0.1584	0.6153	0.49389
Eigenvalue	3.9424	1.3687	1.158	3.8318	1.1756	1.0567
Difference	2.5737	0.2108	0.2729	2.6562	0.1189	0.0937
Proportion	0.3942	0.1369	0.1158	0.3832	0.1176	0.1057
Cumulative	0.3942	0.5311	0.6469	0.3832	0.5007	0.6064

Chapter 6

Difference of Means Test on Organizational Culture Questions

Chapter 5 examined the factor pattern of the 21 cabinet agencies to see if the cultural questions changed during the NPR time period. Although I expected to see change in the cultural questions during the NPR time period, such change was observed in only three agencies (the Departments of Navy, Agriculture, Transportation); within these departments the relationship of customer service to awards and employee skills was more positive and direct in 1996.

Also upon examining each individual question on culture I would expect a higher degree of concurrence on the cultural questions if the goals of NPR were accomplished. Since I have two samples (1992 and 1996) and, I wanted to know whether the means for one sample differ significantly from those of the other sample, the appropriate statistical technique (to test samples concerning means) is the difference of means procedure. The difference of means measured higher or lower degrees of concurrence on how employees view the cultural question during the NPR time period. This chapter examines the results of the difference of means test on the eight cultural questions for each of the 21 cabinet agencies.

Fairness in Awards System

As reported earlier, the factor pattern structure of the 21 agencies shows that customer service" is inversely related to "fairness in awards" within a number of federal agencies. For the Departments of State, Transportation, Housing and Urban Development and the EPA this trend is also supported by the difference of means test results. For example in Table 6-2 the null hypothesis (no difference in employee attitudes on fairness in awards) is rejected at the .005 level in the Departments of State, Housing and Urban Development, Transportation, and the EPA. In the Department of State, for example, the average response to the question on awards decreased from 3.14 to 3.56 at .005 level of significance; in HUD the average response decreased from 3.10 to 3.45 at .005 level of significance; in Transportation the average response decreased from 3.01 to 3. 32 at .005 level of significance; and in EPA the average response decreased from 2.75 to 3.12 at .005 level of significance.

These results could mean that in these agencies the system of awards is perceived as less fair than in 1992. This finding may further explain why there was a stronger inverse relationship between customer service and awards within HUD and Transportation in 1996.

In contrast to these agencies the difference of means test for the Department of the Navy and the Small Business Administration shows that employees may believe that they are more fairly rewarded. For example, in the Navy Department the average response to the awards question increased from 3.40 to 3.17 at .005 level of significance; in SBA the average response to the awards question increased from 3.23 to 2.81 at .005 level of significance. This finding is also supported in the factor pattern structure of these two agencies. For Navy and SBA the relationship of customer service to awards had changed during the NPR time period. Given this result future research could examine how the NPR or internal agency management may have improved the awards system of these two federal cabinet agencies.

Changes in Employee Skills

As reported in Chapter 5 the factor analysis shows that employee skills are inversely related to customer service and awards in a number of federal agencies. These agencies include: the Departments of Commerce, Energy, Housing and Urban Development, Labor, Transportation, the Office of Personnel Management and the Small Business Administration. In Table 6-2 the difference of means test may explain why the responses to "I have the skills to do my job" are inverse to customer service and fairness in awards; in 17 of the federal agencies the null hypotheses (no difference in how federal employees see that they "have the skills to do their job") is rejected at the .005 level of significance. For example, in Agriculture the average response decreased from 2.24 to 3.06; in Commerce the average response decreased from 2.30 to 2.85; in the Air Force the average response decreased from 2.29 to 2.89; in Army the average response decreased from 2.21 to 2.78; in Navy the average response decreased from 2.30 to 2.96; in Education the average response decreased from 2.49 to 3.05; in Energy the average response decreased from 2.38 to 3.89; in EPA the average response decreased from 2.23 to 2.90; in GSA the average response decreased from 2.31 to 2.77; in HHS the average response decreased from 2.33 to 3.12; in Justice the average response decreased

Table 6-1.

Difference of Means Test on Cultural Question "I am awarded fairly"

Agency	$\bar{x}$ - 1992	$\bar{x}$ - 1996	T value	Degrees of Freedom	Level of Significance[2]
Agriculture	3.13	3.38	-2.98	1121	***
Commerce	2.93	2.95	-0.26	819	
Air Force	3.13	3.2	-0.94	989	
Army	3.08	3.16	-0.41	1190	
Navy	3.4	3.17	3.34	982	***
Education	2.91	3.41	-4.4	562	***
Energy	3.26	3.1	0.84	894	
EPA	2.75	3.12	-3.42	390	***
GSA	3.05	3.1	-0.48	860	
HHS	2.97	3.49	-5.27	758	****
HUD	3.1	3.45	-3.05	522	***
Interior	3.1	3.54	-4.75	794	***
Justice	3.03	3.18	-2.2	1058	*
Labor	3.24	3.25	-0.15	757	
NASA	2.81	2.88	-0.85	860	
OPM	2.93	3.59	-5.83	414	***
SBA	3.23	2.81	4.72	865	***
State	3.14	3.56	-5.14	979	***
Transportation	3.01	3.32	-3.3	771	***
Treasury	3.01	3.08	-0.77	875	
VA	2.94	3.27	-2.89	596	***

Table 6-2.

Difference of Means Test on Cultural Question "Job makes good use of skills".

Agency	x̄ - 1992	x̄ - 1996	T value	Degrees of Freedom	Level of Significance[1]
Agriculture	2.24	3.06	-11.66	1157	***
Commerce	2.30	2.85	-6.71	823	***
Air Force	2.29	2.89	-8.82	1033	***
Army	2.21	2.78	-8.46	1092	***
Navy	2.30	2.96	-9.13	840	***
Education	2.49	3.05	-5.67	590	***
Energy	2.38	2.89	-6.45	866	***
EPA	2.23	2.9	-7.23	398	***
GSA	2.31	2.77	-5.94	887	***
HHS	2.33	3.12	-9.31	785	***
HUD	2.40	3.13	-1.24	77	
Interior	2.37	3.03	-8.49	683	***
Justice	2.27	3.13	-12.09	1020	***
Labor	2.26	2.95	-8.24	746	***
NASA	2.06	2.68	-8.18	872	***
OPM	2.40	2.91	-5.24	860	
SBA	2.21	2.92	-16	838	
State	2.20	3.18	-13.55	973	***
Transportation	2.38	3.15	-9.24	783	***
Treasury	2.20	2.84	-8.36	996	***
VA	2.24	3.05	-8.58	627	***

from 2.27 to 3.13; in Labor the average response deceased from 2.26 to 2.95; in Labor the average response decreased from 2.26 to 2.95; in NASA the average response deceased from 2.06 to 2.68; in State the average response decreased from 2.20 to 3.18; in transportation the average response decreased from 2.38 to 3.15; in Treasury the average response decreased from 2.20 to 2.84; and in the VA the average response decreased from 2.24 to 3.05.

From these results I can conclude that in a majority of the federal agencies employees see themselves as having no more skills than in 1992. Such a conclusion may explain why the question employee skills loads inversely to customer service and awards in the factor analysis.

Supervision and Leadership

In analyzing the difference of means test results for the three supervisory cultural questions (Tables 6-3 through 6-5), no significant differences were found in employee "satisfaction" with management within 15 of the cabinet agencies. For the question "supervisor has good leadership skills" (Table 6-3) only three of the 21 cabinet agencies report a significant and positive difference between the two sample populations (NASA, GSA and the Department of Interior). In NASA, the average response on the question "my supervisor has leadership skills" increased from 2.66 to 2.41 at a .005 level of significance; in GSA the average response increased from 2.78 to 2.60 at a .05 level of significance; and in the Department of Interior the average response increased from 2.90 to 2.69 at a .05 level of significance.

For the management question, "my supervisor organizes the work group effectively" (Table 6-4) significant change was observed in three agencies (the Departments of Energy, Interior, and NASA). For example, in the Department of Energy the average response on this question increased from 2.88 to 2.66 at a .01 level of significance; for Interior the average response increased from 2.91 to 2.75 at a .05 level of significance; and in NASA the average response increased from 2.71 to 2.48 at a .005 level of significance. In contrast to these agencies employees see their supervisor as less organized in the Departments of Agriculture, State and the Office of Personnel Management. In the Department of Agriculture the average response for this question decreased from 2.69 to 2.95 at a .005 level of significance; in OPM the average response decreased from 2.65 to 2.93 at a .005 level of significance; and in the State Department the average response decreased from 2.79 to 2.99 at a .01 level of significance.

Finally for the question "I am satisfied with my supervisor" (Table 6-5) there 44 is no overall increase in satisfaction with supervision for 19 of the agencies. In two of the agencies (Agriculture and OPM) respondents were less satisfied with their supervisor at a .05 level of significance. In Agriculture the average response to this question decreased from 2.43 to 2.61; and in OPM the average response decreased from 2.51 to 2.72.

In summary although the difference of means test does show that agency management has changed within a few agencies, the overall conclusion from the data found in Tables 6-3 through 6-5 does not show that leadership and supervision have improved during the NPR implementation period.

Cooperation and Teamwork

The results of the difference of means test support the conclusions of the literature that teamwork is an important variable in defining organizational culture. In comparing the difference of means test results of all of the cultural questions, the teamwork variable was the only dimension where culture had changed in any meaningful way (9 of the 21 cabinet agencies). This conclusion is also supported in more recent studies where the "team orientation" was found to be a pervasive organizational culture theme (Hofstede et al.,1990; O'Reilly et al., 1991; and, Chatman and Jehn, 1994).

In this research I found that in 9 of the 21 agencies (Table 6-6) the null hypothesis on the teamwork question is rejected at levels of .05 and less (no difference in how employees perceive teamwork and cooperation in their work unit). For example, in Agriculture the average response increased from 2.47 to 2.33 at a .05 level of significance; in Army the average response increased from 2.54 to 2.33 at a .005 level of significance; in Navy the average response increased from 2.60 to 2.45 at a .05 level of significance; in Education the average response increased from 2.72 to 2.52 at a .05 level of significance; in Energy the average response increased from 2.57 to 3.35 at .005 level of significance; in EPA the average response increased from 2.43 to 2.29 at .05 level of significance; in HUD the average response increased from 2.44 to 2.44 at .05 level of significance; in Interior the average response increased from 2.72 to 2.48 at .005 level

Table 6-3.

Difference of Means Test on Cultural Question "My supervisor has leadership skills"

Agency	x̄ - 1992	x̄ - 1996	T value	Degrees of Freedom	Level of Significance[1]
Agriculture	2.65	2.85	-2.62	1164	**
Commerce	2.81	2.68	1.44	847	
Air Force	2.74	2.68	0.73	1063	
Army	2.74	2.67	1.04	1154	
Navy	2.91	2.77	1.81	910	
Education	2.91	2.94	-0.29	586	
Energy	2.8	2.63	1.88	916	
EPA	2.67	2.57	1.05	463	
GSA	2.78	2.6	2.19	945	*
HHS	2.82	2.89	-0.73	830	
HUD	2.88	2.74	1.36	509	
Interior	2.9	2.69	2.46	892	*
Justice	2.81	2.81	-0.06	1032	
Labor	2.75	2.67	0.92	790	
NASA	2.66	2.41	2.98	893	***
OPM	2.76	2.93	-1.63	460	
SBA	2.77	2.77	-0.02	859	
State	2.72	2.88	-1.92	1002	
Transportation	2.67	2.63	0.52	831	
Treasury	2.71	2.7	0.12	1002	
VA	2.77	2.88	-1.1	618	

Table 6-4.

Difference of Means Test on Cultural Question "My supervisor is organized".

Agency	x̄ - 1992	x̄ - 1996	T value	Degrees of Freedom	Level of Significance[1]
Agriculture	2.69	2.95	-3.55	1157	***
Commerce	2.82	2.72	1.24	848	
Air Force	2.83	2.79	0.5	1028	
Army	2.82	2.74	1.16	1143	
Navy	2.96	2.91	0.69	886	
Education	2.99	3.01	-0.28	582	
Energy	2.88	2.66	2.67	902	**
EPA	2.74	2.64	1.05	425	
GSA	2.81	2.73	0.99	915	
HHS	2.91	2.97	-0.57	799	
HUD	2.98	2.85	1.17	483	
Interior	2.81	2.75	2.08	911	*
Justice	2.88	2.85	0.4	1032	
Labor	2.81	2.75	0.67	781	
NASA	2.71	2.48	2.92	892	***
OPM	2.65	2.93	-2.93	457	***
SBA	2.76	2.91	-1.81	849	
State	2.79	2.99	-2.64	991	**
Transportation	2.65	2.76	-1.45	799	
Treasury	2.78	2.82	-0.47	1008	
VA	2.77	2.82	-0.54	624	

Table 6-5. Difference of Means Test on Cultural Question
"I am satisfied with my supervisor"

Agency	x̄ - 1992	x̄ - 1996	T value	Degrees of Freedom	Level of Significance[1]
Agriculture	2.43	2.61	-2.4	1160	*
Commerce	2.53	2.48	0.58	848	
Air Force	2.53	2.51	0.24	1006	
Army	2.52	2.47	0.76	1114	
Navy	2.62	2.59	0.4	892	
Education	2.58	2.6	-0.19	604	
Energy	2.5	2.38	1.61	927	
EPA	2.4	2.35	0.57	460	
GSA	2.52	2.42	1.28	928	
HHS	2.58	2.67	-1.01	806	
HUD	2.6	2.55	0.54	5120	
Interior	2.62	2.47	1.76	899	
Justice	2.55	2.6	-0.69	1038	
Labor	2.58	2.46	1.36	776	
NASA	2.39	2.29	1.34	892	
OPM	2.51	2.72	-2.18	434	*
SBA	2.49	2.52	-0.3	859	
State	2.51	2.66	-1.94	992	
Transportation	2.42	2.47	-0.6	799	
Treasury	2.52	2.48	0.58	1013	
VA	2.46	2.63	-1.73	631	

Table 6-6.

Difference of Means Test on Cultural Question "There is a spirit of team work and cooperation in my work unit."

Agency	$\bar{x}$ - 1992	$\bar{x}$ - 1996	T value	Degrees of Freedom	Level of Significance[1]
Agriculture	2.47	2.33	2.26	1171	*
Commerce	2.43	2.35	0.93	832	
Air Force	2.53	2.43	1.58	1031	
Army	2.54	2.33	3.2	1130	***
Navy	2.6	2.45	2.14	877	*
Education	2.72	2.52	2.05	615	*
Energy	2.57	2.35	2.93	909	***
EPA	2.43	2.29	1.65	465	*
GSA	2.56	2.43	1.68	885	
HHS	2.64	2.56	0.91	799	
HUD	2.66	2.44	2.53	550	*
Interior	2.72	2.48	3.02	896	***
Justice	2.58	2.44	1.88	1049	
Labor	2.63	2.5	1.42	770	
NASA	2.3	2.14	2.33	885	*
OPM	2.61	2.48	1.37	422	
SBA	2.43	2.38	0 .78	856	
State	2.43	2.54	-1.49	986	
Transportation	2.53	2.5	0 .25	766	
Treasury	2.6	2.49	1.52	992	
VA	2.45	2.49	-0.39	639	

of significance; and in NASA the average response increased from 2.30 to 2.14 at a .05 level of significance;

In comparing the teamwork question to the other seven questions, I conclude that teamwork may be the only dimension of organizational culture that changed between 1992 and 1996. This result leads us to reject the null hypothesis and conclude that a cooperative-participative culture could have emerged as the result of NPR implementation.

Freedom in Work

Reinventing government and the NPR rests on the assumption that an entrepreneurial, "bottom-up" culture can be created to serve and support the bureaucracy. In this research the following hypothesis was posed to determine if the NPR created such a "bottom-up" decision making culture: has the National Performance Review improved the problem solving and decision making processes within the federal cabinet agencies? Accordingly, question 33 ("I have independence in how I do my work," 1992 MSPB survey), and question 22 (I have been given more flexibility in how I accomplish my work," 1996 survey) were used from the Merit Board survey to accept or reject the proposed hypothesis.

In comparing the two sample means to these questions in 1992 and 1996 the difference of means tests shows (Table 6-7) that the respondents perceive having less flexibility than before. In 19 of the federal agencies the null hypothesis is rejected at a .005 level of significance. For example in Agriculture the average response decreased from 2.11 to 2.86; in Commerce the average response decreased from 2.04 to 2.74; in the Air Force the average response decreased from 2.18 to 2.79; in Army the average response decreased from 2.16 to 2.70; in Navy the average response decreased from 2.22 to 2.72; in Education the average response decreased from 2.22 to 2.80; in Energy the average response decreased from 2.23 to 2.66; in EPA the average response decreased from 2.04 to 2.78; in GSA the average response decreased from 2.20 to 2.50; in HHS the average response decreased from 2.28 to 2.96; in HUD the average response decreased from 2.22 to 2.64; in Justice the average response decreased from 2.37 to 2.89; in Labor the average response deceased from 2.26 to 2.95; in Labor the average response decreased from 2.37 to 2.89; in NASA the average response deceased from 1.91 to 2.62; in OPM the average response decreased from 2.12 to 2.77; in SBA the average response decreased form 2.14 to 2.92; in State the average response decreased from 2.33 to 3.01; in Transportation the average response decreasedfrom 2.29 to 2.90; in Treasury the average response decreased from 2.16 to 2.76; and in the VA the average response decreased from 2.22 to 2.85.

One of the goals of the NPR was to reduce the regulations that stifle managers and employees; the difference of means test results show that employees do not perceive that the NPR provided them with any more flexibility than in 1992. Perhaps this perception is supported by the fact that as each agency was downsized, the jobs of the federal work force were "enlarged" with more responsibility. Future research might examine the effects of such factors when one of the proposed cultural improvements is "empowerment" of the work force.

Customer Service

The results of the difference of means test on the cultural questions for "customer service" produced an analogous finding to the "flexibility" question (Table 6-8). In 19 of the agencies the null hypothesis is rejected at a level of.005 (the only exception being the Department of Education). For example, in Agriculture the average response decreased from 2.30 to 3.95; in Commerce the average response decreased from 2.16 to 3.86; in the Air Force the average response decreased from 2.12 to 4.36; in Army the average response decreased from 2.05 to 4.13; in Navy the average response decreased from 2.14 to 4.25; in Education the average response decreased from 2.44 to 3.44; in Energy the average response decreased from 2.28 to 3.72; in GSA the average response decreased from 2.21 to 3.34; in HHS the average response decreased from 2.30 to 3.89; in HUD the average response decreased from 2.46 to 3.25; in Interior the average response decreased from 2.50 to 3.80; in Justice the average response decreased from 2.30 to 3.87; in Labor the average response deceased from 2.39 to 4.22; in NASA the average response deceased from 2.12 to 3.99; in OPM the average response decreased from 2.14 to 3.63; in SBA the average response decreased form 2.15 to 3.80; in State the average response decreased from 2.24 to 3.97; in Transportation the average response decreased from 2.29 to 4.06; in Treasury the average response decreased from 2.26 to 3.80; and in the VA the average response decreased from 2.25 to 3.93.

From these results I can conclude that employees believe less, than in 1992, that customer service has improved. Since improved customer service is an important assumption of the NPR the difference of means test results show that there is less agreement that the "customer is satisfied" than in 1992. In Chapter 7 I will compare this finding to both

Table 6-7.

Difference of Means Test on Cultural Question "I have independence in how I do my work"

Agency	x̄ - 1992	x̄ - 1996	T value	Degrees of Freedom	Level of Significance[1]
Agriculture	2.11	2.86	-11.99	1111	***
Commerce	2.04	2.74	-9.69	743	***
Air Force	2.18	2.79	-9.72	839	***
Army	2.16	2.7	-8.73	963	***
Navy	2.22	2.72	-7.75	841	***
Education	2.22	2.8	-6.14	519	***
Energy	2.23	2.66	-6.04	809	***
EPA	2.04	2.78	-8.12	335	***
GSA	2.2	2.5	-4.3	811	***
HHS	2.28	2.96	-8.4	722	***
HUD	2.22	2.64	-4.89	626	
Interior	2.28	2.18	1.36	920	
Justice	2.1	2.73	-10.18	976	***
Labor	2.37	2.89	-6.28	683	***
NASA	1.91	2.62	-10.68	792	***
OPM	2.12	2.77	-7.01	376	***
SBA	2.14	2.92	-10.85	721	***
State	2.33	3.01	-. 9.87	923	***
Transportation	2.29	2.9	-8.03	761	***
Treasury	2.16	2.76	-8.86	928	***
VA	2.22	2.85	-7.01	649	***

Table 6-8.
Difference of Means Test on Cultural Question "Work Unit
Customers are satisfied."

Agency	x̄ - 1992	x̄ - 1996	T value	Degrees of Freedom	Level of Significance[1]
Agriculture	2.3	3.95	-23.93	1002	***
Commerce	2.16	3.86	-19.85	625	***
Air Force	2.12	4.36	-32.22	683	***
Army	2.05	4.13	-29.65	745	***
Navy	2.14	4.25	-26.91	613	***
Education	2.44	3.44	2.05	615	*
Energy	2.28	3.72	-17.6	619	***
EPA	2.3	3.8	1.65	465	
GSA	2.21	3.34	-15.6	659	***
HHS	2.3	3.89	-17.66	611	***
HUD	2.46	3.25	-8.12	390	***
Interior	2.5	3.8	-15.54	657	***
Justice	2.3	3.87	-21.6	821	***
Labor	2.39	4.22	-19.74	563	***
NASA	2.12	3.99	-24.24	671	***
OPM	2.14	3.63	-15.03	321	***
SBA	2.15	3.8	-20.82	585	***
State	2.24	3.97	-24.35	755	***
Transportation	2.29	4.06	-21.81	573	***
Treasury	2.26	3.8	-19.27	743	***
VA	2.25	3.93	-17.83	665	***

Carroll (1994) and Thompson and Jones' (1995) conclusions on the National Performance Review.

Also as stated in Chapter 5 there is an inverse relationship between customer service and awards within four agencies in 1992. This occurred in the Departments of State, Treasury, Housing and Urban Development and the Small Business Administration. This inverse relationship can be interpreted to mean that even when customers are served well, employees may not be rewarded for such efforts. This result will be discussed in Chapter 7.

Chapter 7

Discussion

This study contributes to the current literature on organizational culture in two ways. First, there is very limited use of factor analysis models in the organizational science literature. When used to examine organizational culture these studies have tended, with rare exceptions, to use standardized questionnaires to assess culture (Hofstede, Neuijen, Ohayv and Sanders, 1990; O'Reilly, Chatman and Caldwell, 1991; Chatman and Jehn, 1994; Thomas, Shankster and Mathieu, 1994). Only one of these studies (Thomas, Shankster and Mathieu, 1994) addressed supervision and leadership in the factor model. However, Thomas, Shankster, and Mathieu did not examine the effects of leadership on culture. In this research three sources of the effects of leadership were examined in order to expand understanding regarding organizational culture and change within the context of the NPR. These were: (1) satisfaction with supervisor; (2) supervisor organizes the work group effectively; and, (3) supervisor has good leadership skills.

The second contribution is how I studied the factors relating organizational culture and change. In only one study (Chatman and Jehn, 1994) were factor analysis methods used to study patterns of organizational culture. However, this study did not assess organizational culture across time, the approach taken in this research.

As stated in Chapter 5 the cumulative eigenvalues produced in the principal factor analysis were used to test the efficacy of the cultural questions over time (Table 5-1). Concurrent with this analysis, an examination is made of the federal agencies where change is noted, and how the explanatory variables load in each factor dimension. In this chapter I will compare the results of the factor analysis and difference of means test to answer the proposed research question: has the NPR changed the organizational culture of the federal cabinet agencies?

From the results of the difference of means test we can conclude that minimal change is evidenced in a majority of the federal agencies for the ten organizational culture questions. One conclusion from the difference of means test is that there is 43 percent less concurrence on the cultural questions across the 21 federal cabinet agencies (73 of 168 questions show less concurrence on the cultural question in the difference of means test). This conclusion is also supported by the cumulative eigenvalues obtained on the 21 cabinet agencies over time

(Table 5-1).   This table also shows that the overall efficacy of the
organizational cultural questions remained constant in 19 of the cabinet
agencies.   These findings are also supported by the focus interviews
(Table 4-1).   The NPR staff report sporadic change in only 8 of the 21
federal cabinet agencies.   These results allow for acceptance of the null
hypothesis (that the NPR did not change the culture of the federal
cabinet agencies).   They may also support the idea that the NPR is
simply administrative theory driven by "budgetary politics" and not
bringing any real change or limited change--it is not apparent in every
agency.

A.   Cooperation and Teamwork

Osborne and Gaebler's reinventing government suggests that today's
public administrator uses the principles of "teamwork" to overcome the
productivity barriers associated with government bureaucracies.   The
concept of "teamwork" dates back to Roethlisberger and Dickson's
(1939) account of the Hawthorne Experiments.   In describing an
organization's social system, the early human relationist writers
(Roethlisberger and Dickson, 1939; Benne, 1943; and Triste, 1985)
illustrated how a group (or team) evolved its own set of norms and
values.   Their research illustrated how these norms and values affected
the behavior and performance of individual team members.   The
importance of "teams" within organizations remained a central point in
the field of management through the 1980s (Argyris, 1973a, 1973b,
1982, 1992; Benne, Bradford, Gibb and Lippitt, 1975; Bennis, 1993;
McGregor, 1960; Oakley and Krug, 1993; Presthus, 1978; Shepard,
1958; and Tannenbaum, 1954).
   The results of the difference of means test support the conclusions of
the literature that teamwork is an important variable in defining
organizational culture.   In comparing the difference of means test results
of all of the cultural questions, the teamwork variable was the only
dimension where culture had changed in any substantive way (one-third
of the 21 cabinet agencies).   This conclusion is also supported in more
recent studies where the "team orientation" was found to be a pervasive
organizational culture theme (Hofstede et al.,1990; O'Reilly et al., 1991;
and, Chatman and Jehn, 1994).
   In Table 6-6 I found that in 9 of the 21 agencies, the null hypothesis
on the teamwork question is rejected at levels of .05 and less (no
difference in how employees perceive teamwork and cooperation in

their work unit). These agencies include the Departments of Agriculture, Army, Navy, Education, Energy, Housing and Urban Development, Interior, NASA, and EPA. This result leads us to conclude that a cooperative-participative culture has emerged in the 21 federal cabinet agencies since implementation of the NPR. The results on the teamwork question are more compelling based on the fact that the federal cabinet agencies underwent a major "downsizing" of staff from 1993 through 1996 (Table 8-2). In view of this result how could eight cabinet agencies enhance teamwork and cooperation while downsizing a major segment of its staff? Future research could examine the effects of teamwork during downsizing.

Upon comparing the results of the factor analysis to the difference of means test procedure other patterns emerge with respect to the cultural questions. For example, in the Department of Education the predictability of the organizational culture questions increased higher in this agency than in the remaining agencies (an increase in 4 percent from 1992). As stated earlier the Department of Navy was the only agency to show significant change in how employees perceive the agency's award system. Finally, NASA shows a significant difference of the samples of respondents to the greatest number of cultural questions than any other agency (In NASA employees more strongly agree that their manager is a "leader", and is "organized." NASA employees also agree that there is more teamwork than in 1992). Future research could examine how changes in agency leadership and the agency's awards system may effect the climate of teamwork in the work place.

B. A New Customer Driven Culture

In the factor analysis results for all of the federal agencies (Tables 5-2 to 5-22) I have labeled Factor 2 in the 1996 data as "NPR improving customer service." In fourteen of the federal agencies this question loads high in Factor 2.

As noted earlier one of the principal goals of reinventing government is that today's public organization must be flexible, adaptive and responsive to the "needs" of the citizen or "customer." The results of the data refute the picture of a federal civil service that has uniformly accepted the assumptions of Osborne and Gaebler and Peters and Waterman (1982) that customer orientation is important. Perhaps this finding is best explained by Carroll's (1995) position that the NPR's emphasis on customer satisfaction cannot apply to government.

According to Carroll, the fact is that "most federal responsibilities and functions" do not exist to service customers. The data support this position in Table 6-8 and shows rejection of the null hypothesis at a .005 level of significance within 18 agencies (employees believe less, than in 1992, that customer service has improved).

Another possible explanation of the results on customer service is seen in the differential wording of the customer service question in 1992 and 1996. For example, in 1992 customer service was measured by the question "work unit customers satisfied with quality". In 1996 the service question was changed to "NPR has improved customer service." Given the differential wording of the questions agency employees could be evaluating customer service from two different perspectives (customer satisfaction versus the NPR's effect on customer service). Hence, two different mean responses could have been compared on customer service resulting in a Type 1 error. It is possible that a true null hypothesis may have been rejected allowing me to conclude employees did not see improved customer service.

In spite of these assumptions the difference of means test shows that DOE employees perceive improved customer service in 1996. This coincides with the observed change in the cumulative eigenvalues for the Department of Education; the efficacy of the cultural questions for DOE increased by 4 percent from 1992 to 1996.

For two agencies (EPA and Interior) there was no significant change in the difference of means test for the "customer service" question. However, in these two agencies, the average response on the teamwork increased at a .05 level of significance. Also in the Department of Interior employees believed that their managers improved in leadership and work group organization. Future research could explore the effects of teamwork and supervision on customer satisfaction.

Finally, there is an inverse relationship between customer service and rewards question within four agencies in 1992. In these four cases "fairness in awards" had a negative correlation value to the common factor; while "unit customers satisfied with quality" had a positive correlation to the common factor. This inverse relationship can be interpreted to mean that as customers are served well, employees are not awarded. This conclusion runs counter to all motivation theories and reinventing government; reinventing government supports the development of reward systems that ultimately improve customer service. A further review of the 1992 survey does not reveal flaws in the questionnaire construction (i.e., a reversal in the Likert scale to each question).

C. Leadership and Supervision.

Within the factor analysis matrix for all federal agencies I have labeled Factor 1 as Supervision and Leadership. This factor includes the following predicator variables: (1) satisfaction with supervisor; (2) supervisor organizes the work group effectively; and, (3) supervisor has good leadership skills.

From Tables 6-3 to 6-5 I conclude that there are no significant differences in the mean responses to the three cultural questions on agency management and leadership. In three of the federal agencies (Interior, the General Services Administration and NASA) the difference of means test supports the literature's assumptions on the effects of leadership. According to Bellavita (1989), Geier (1991) and Covey (1991) the actions of top management have a major impact on an organization's culture. Also in three studies (Adams, 1991; Raturi, 1992; and Biggerstaff, 1990) leadership was found to play an important role in developing an organization's culture.

For the question "My supervisor is organized" employees see their supervisor as more organized in 1996 for the Departments of Energy, Interior, and NASA. For the question "supervisor has good leadership skills" only three of the 21 cabinet agencies report a significant, positive difference between the two sample populations (GSA, NASA and the Department of Interior).

For the remaining 18 federal agencies there are no significant differences in the sample population means in 1992 and 1996. In three agencies (the Departments of Agriculture, State and the Office of Personnel Management) employees see their supervisor as less organized than in 1992. In the Department of Agriculture employees see their supervisor as exhibiting less leadership ability than before. Except for OPM, the observed changes from the difference of means test cannot be explained by the agency field interviews. For the Office of Personnel Management the difference of means test shows that employees see their managers as less organized; also, they are also less satisfied with these managers. Perhaps this finding is best explained that from 1993 to 1996 OPM reduced its staff by 43 percent (the greatest downsized agency in the federal government). One may question whether OPM employee dissatisfaction with management may be related to agency downsizing. Future research could examine the effects of the manager's role in a downsizing effort.

D. Cultural Questions Where Change is Not Supported

Osborne and Gaebler state, "What we need most if this revolution is to succeed... is a new framework for understanding a government, a new way of thinking about government" (Osborne and Gaebler, 1992, p. 321). The new way of thinking advocated by Osborne and Gaebler reflects the writings of the organization as an interactive "learning system" adaptive to change and forces internal and external to the organization (Argyris 1973; 1982; 1993). Also the writings of Senge (1990, 1994) and Srivastva and Cooperrider (1990) on "action learning" and "appreciation management" build on the Argyris model of the learning organization. This new way of thinking about government requires employees to be current in skills critical to high performance and an organizational culture where they will be free to practice those skills.

In   Table 6-2 the difference of means test may explain why the responses to "I have the skills to do my job" are inverse to customer service and fairness in awards; in 17 of the federal agencies the null hypotheses (no difference in how federal employees see that they "have the skills to do their job") is rejected at the .005 level. From this data we find that a majority of employees see themselves as having no more skills than in 1992. Hence, we can reject Hypothesis 3 and conclude that the NPR has not reinvented the federal bureaucracy into a culture of improved creativity and problem solving.

Reinventing government and the NPR also rest on the assumption that an entrepreneurial, bottom-up culture can be created to serve and support the bureaucracy. This research sought to determine if the NPR has created such an entrepreneurial culture within the federal cabinet agencies. Accordingly, question 33 ("I have independence in how I do my work," 1992 MSPB survey), and question 22 (I have been given more flexibility in how I accomplish my work," 1996 survey) were used from the Merit Board survey to accept or reject the proposed hypothesis.

In comparing the two sample means on the independence/flexibility question the difference of means test shows (Table 6-7) employees having less job flexibility in 1996. In every agency the null hypothesis is rejected at the .005 level. The results of the difference of means test for this question supports the conclusion that the NPR has not created an entrepreneurial, bottom-up culture within the federal cabinet agencies. This data suggest that the change as outlined by Bennis (1966, 1993) and Osborne and Gaebler (1992) has not occurred in the federal cabinet agencies. These authors believe that organizations in the next reform period of management need to be marked by less hierarchy and functional specialization.

This research asked the question: why did federal employees perceive having less flexibility in their jobs in 1996? Perhaps this can be explained by the obstacles experienced in the NPR process (Thompson,1996; and Shoop, 1994). According to Thompson one obstacle to change was in the "old bureaucratic system." According to Thompson, Al Gore sees the "old bureaucratic system" as a major obstacle to change sought in the NPR process. According to Gore, the traditional bureaucracy became a "blob that kept coming back... as a character in a horror movie" (Thompson, 1996, 40).

Shoop (1994) further describes the obstacles of a bureaucracy with his example from the Department of Army's reinvention labs. According to Shoop these and other labs were often met with bureaucratic roadblocks created by department staff. According to Shoop,

"An official from and Army Research and Development Lab took up Gore's challenge, complaining that plans to implement more flexible personnel policies at the R&D labs were being held up in staff offices at the Pentagon. The official pointed the finger at political appointees in charge of those offices, telling Gore that while he was encouraging others to break through barriers, 'your own people are saying no' (Shoop, 1994, 42).

From these examples it is clear that future change efforts must address ways to make the bureaucracy supportive when the goal is to empower employee decision making.

Chapter 8

Conclusions

In 1992 President Bill Clinton delegated the responsibility to develop a new management culture within the national government. In 1993 and 1994 the Gore Task Force produced NPR I and NPR II, reports which outlined the plans to and results of reinventing the national government.

This book analyzed whether the implementation of the National Performance Review (NPR) improved the culture of the federal cabinet agencies. A combined quantitative/qualitative analysis found that there is no evidence to suggest that the organizational culture of the federal cabinet agencies has changed. This conclusion is supported by the factor analysis results and the difference of means tests performed on the cultural questions for each of the 21 cabinet agencies over time. This finding is supported in Table 8-1 which shows less concurrence on 43 percent of the cultural questions within the 21 cabinet agencies. The conclusion that there is no discernable cultural change during the NPR time period is also supported by the agency focus interviews (Table 4-1).

Although the results of the factor analysis and difference of means test show no change on most of the cultural questions within the federal government, employees in nine agencies perceive greater teamwork in 1996. This conclusion is supported in the summary of the difference of means test results for all of the cabinet agencies in Table 8-1. In addition the difference of means test shows that in the Departments of Navy, Interior and NASA there is cultural change on the questions relating to leadership, supervision and rewards.

Table 8-1.

Summary of Difference of Means Tests on Organizational Culture Questions[3]

Agency	Freedom	Manager is Leader	Mgr. is Organized	Satisfied with Mgr.	Teamwork	Awards	Customer Service	Skills
Agriculture	Negative	Negative	Negative	Negative	Positive	Negative	Negative	Negative
Commerce	Negative						Negative	Negative
Army	Negative				Positive	Positive	Negative	Negative
Navy	Negative				Positive		Negative	Negative
Education	Negative		Positive		Positive	Negative	Positive	Negative
Energy	Negative				Positive		Negative	Negative
EPA	Negative					Negative		
GSA	Negative					Negative	Negative	Negative
HHS	Negative					Negative	Negative	Negative
HUD					Positive	Negative	Negative	Negative
Interior		Positive	Positive		Positive	Negative	Negative	Negative
Justice	Negative						Negative	Negative
Labor	Negative						Negative	Negative
NASA	Negative	Positive	Positive		Positive		Negative	Negative
OPM	Negative		Negative	Negative		Negative	Negative	
SBA	Negative					Positive	Negative	
State	Negative		Negative			Negative	Negative	Negative
DOT	Negative					Negative	Negative	Negative
Treasury	Negative						Negative	Negative
VA	Negative					Negative	Negative	Negative
Air Force	Negative						Negative	Negative

Inventing a New Learning Culture

Reinventing government seeks to transform the culture of the modern bureaucracy from thinking and acting "out of the box" into a "new way of thinking within government." This new way of thinking portrays today's public bureaucracy as a highly interactive "learning system" adaptive to forces, both internal and external to the organization (Osborne and Gaebler, 1992; Argyris 1973; 1982; 1993; Senge 1990, 1994; and Srivastva and Cooperrider 1990). As today's public bureaucracy evolves into this new learning organization the public service must improve in skill and knowledge.

An examination of the factor pattern structure for the questions "Unit customers satisfied with quality" and "I have the skills needed to do my job" shows an inverse relationship between these questions in 1996. The inverse relationship between these questions occurred in the Departments of Labor and Commerce, the Office of Personnel Management and the Small Business Administration. In Table 6-2 the difference of means test may explain the nature of this inverse relationship; in 17 of the federal agencies the null hypotheses (no difference in how federal employees see that they "have the skills to do their job") is rejected at the .005 level. From this result we can conclude that in a majority of the federal agencies employees see themselves as having no more skills than in 1992. Based on this data we can reject the research question hat the NPR has not reinvented the federal bureaucracy by developing employee skills, improving the creativity and problem solving capacities of the federal cabinet agencies.

Teamwork

Osborne and Gaebler's reinventing government suggests that today's public administrator uses the principles of "teamwork" to overcome the productivity barriers associated with government bureaucracies. In this book (Table 6-6) we find that in nine of the 21 agencies the null hypothesis on the teamwork question is rejected at levels of .05 and less (no difference in how employees perceive teamwork and cooperation in their work unit). These agencies include the Departments of Agriculture, Army, Navy, Education, Housing and Urban Development, Interior, NASA, and EPA.

The results of the difference of means test support the conclusions of the literature that teamwork is an important variable in defining organizational culture (Argyris, 1973a, 1973b, 1982, 1992; Benne, Bradford, Gibb and Lippitt, 1975; Bennis, 1993; McGregor, 1960; Oakley and Krug, 1993; Presthus, 1978; Shepard, 1958; and Tannenbaum, 1954). As stated earlier the Department of Navy was the only agency to show significant change in how employees perceive the agency's award system. Also NASA shows a significant difference of the samples of respondents to the greatest number of cultural questions than in any other agency (NASA employees more strongly agree that their manager is a "leader", and is "organized." NASA employees also agree that there is more teamwork than in 1992). Future research could examine how changes in agency leadership and the agency's awards system may effect the climate of teamwork in the work place.

Transforming the Bureaucracy

Reinventing government and the NPR rest on the assumption that an entrepreneurial, bottom-up culture can be created to serve and support the bureaucracy. This book sought to determine if the NPR has created such an entrepreneurial culture within the federal cabinet agencies.

One of the goals of the NPR was to reduce the regulations that stifle managers and employees. Related to this objective is the proposition that by reducing paperwork and regulations employees will be empowered to make decisions. In comparing the two sample means to these questions in 1992 and 1996 the difference of means tests shows (Table 6-7) that the respondents perceive having less flexibility than before. In every agency the null hypothesis is rejected at the .005 level. This data suggest that the change as outlined by Bennis (1966, 1993) and Osborne and Gaebler (1992) has not occurred in the federal cabinet agencies.

The fact that employees perceive having less flexibility in their jobs can be explained by the obstacles experienced in the NPR process (Thompson, 1996; and Shoop, 1994). The bureaucratic roadblocks reported by Thompson and Shoop often stymied attempts to eliminate red tape and delegate decision making downward within the federal agencies. From the data and findings in this book future change efforts must address ways to make the bureaucracy supportive when the goal is to empower employee decision making.

Beginning with Denhart (1981) the literature supports the belief that the pubic manager must play a direct role in reshaping the public bureaucracy (Argyris, 1990; Senge, 1990 and 1994; and Covey, 1991).

Leading Within the Federal Cabinet Agencies

In analyzing the difference of means test results on the supervision and leadership questions there are no significant differences in federal employee "satisfaction" with management between 1992 and 1996 in 19 of the cabinet agencies (Table 6-5). However, in 5 of the federal agencies (Energy, Interior, the General Services Administration and NASA) the difference of means test supports the literature's assumptions on the effects of leadership. For the question "My supervisor is organized" employees see their supervisor as more organized in 1996 for the Departments of Energy, Interior, and NASA (Table 6-4). For the question "supervisor has good leadership skills" only two of the twenty-one cabinet agencies report a significant, positive difference between the two sample populations (Table 6-3, NASA and the Department of Interior). Although the difference of means test does show that agency management has changed within these five agencies, the overall conclusion is that managerial culture change did not occur during the NPR time period.

Except for OPM the observed changes from the difference of means test cannot be explained by the agency field interviews. The difference of means test results for OPM show that employees are less satisfied with their supervisors. Also in OPM employees see their supervisor as less organized than in 1992. Perhaps this finding is best explained by the fact that from 1993 through 1996 OPM reduced its staff by 43 percent (the greatest downsized agency in the federal government as shown in Table 7-2). One may question whether OPM employee dissatisfaction with management may be related to agency downsizing. Future research could examine the effects of the manager's role in a downsizing effort.

Table 8-2. Federal Agency Staffing Trends 1993-1996

Agency	1993 Staff Years	1996 Staff Years	Percent Change	Rank
Agriculture	114,420	105452	-0.07	11.5
Commerce	38343	35842	-0.07	11.5
DOD	2636400	2282000	-0.13	6
Education	4876	4750	-0.03	16.5
Energy	20410	19762	-0.03	16.5
EPA	17479	17416	-0.04	15
GSA	20249	14780	-0.27	2
HHS	64980	58924	-0.1	8
HUD	13294	11628	-0.13	6
Interior	76880	67150	-0.13	6
Justice	83574	95687	0.07	18
Labor	18003	16655	-0.08	10
NASA	25700	21555	-0.16	4
PM	6208	3557	-0.43	1
SBA	5599	4284	-0.24	3
State	26000	23700	-0.09	9
Treasury	161100	153319	-0.05	13.5
VA	234428	223727	-0.05	13.5

Rewards and Recognition

As noted earlier in this book one of the goals of the Gore Report (NPR I) was to improve effectiveness by giving managers the tools "to promote and reward." The results of the data from the difference of means test for the question "fairness in awards" (Table 6-1) refute the assumption that the NPR has improved the awards structure and processes of the federal cabinet agencies. Table 6-1 shows that in four of the agencies the null hypothesis is rejected at a level of.005 (employees believe less, than in 1992, that there is "fairness in rewards"). This result may explain why there was an inverse relationship between the customer service and awards question in the factor pattern structure of these four agencies. These agencies include: the Departments of State, Treasury, Housing and Urban Development and the Small Business Administration. The inverse nature of the relationship between these questions can mean that employees are not rewarded when the customers is served well.

In contrast to these four agencies, three agencies show employees believing that they are more fairly awarded than in 1992 (the Departments of Navy, Air Force and the EPA). Although these results cannot be explained by the agency field interviews, an analysis of the factor pattern structure of these agencies may explain the nature of change observed in the responses to the award question. For example in the Navy Department and the EPA the relationship of the customer service question to "merit awards" became more direct and positive in the 1996 factor loadings (in 1992 the relationship between these questions was inverse). Perhaps in these agencies the institutional reward system was more closely linked to "serving the customer." This contrasts with the four agencies where employees may not see rewards associated with serving the customer. This latter conclusion supports Miller's (1994) belief that the NPR will not work since it operates on a flawed premise; that the successful incentive and reward processes of the private sector can be transferred to the public sector. Shearer (1994) concludes that without accountability and reward systems the NPR goals cannot succeed. From these results it is clear that future research must examine the relationship of merit reward systems to improving culture.

Putting Customers First

The organizational culture variable, "customer service" loads high in Factor 2 for 14 of the 21 agencies in 1996. In contrast in 1992, customer service did not load high in any of the 21 agency factor patterns. These results on the customer service variable hold significance for the field of public administration. Customer or "client" relationships are long recognized in the public administration literature (Ostrom and Ostrom, 1971; and Meier, 1979). These writings state that the public sector should function in a market like environment. Like a business, government must learn to satisfy its customers.

The idea of customer satisfaction was also popularized in Peters and Waterman's 1981 book, In *Search of Excellence.* Osborne and Gaebler (1992) echo Peters and Waterman's satisfying the customer theme. According to Osborne and Gaebler successful public agencies keep their management structure simple and flexible. These organizations also ensure agency accessibility to the taxpayer. If a taxpayer has a complaint, their issue was resolved by the agency.

In my analysis of the factor pattern structure of the 21 cabinet agencies I have shown that the customer service question was inversely related to the merit "award" questions during the study time period for four of the cabinet agencies (the Departments of State, Treasury, Housing and Urban Development and the Small Business Administration). The data support my conclusion that the federal agencies have yet to reinvent an awards system which supports the goal of improved customer service. This conclusion is also supported in the difference of means test for the customer service question; in Table 6-8 for 18 of the agencies the null hypothesis is rejected at a level of .005 (employees believe less, than in 1992, that customer service improvement has improved).

The data also support the belief that the NPR goal of improving "customer service" has marginalized the role of government (Miller, 1994; Carroll, 1995; Fox, 1996, Thompson and Jones, 1995, and Hart and Hart, 1997). The fact that employees in 18 agencies see less customer satisfaction may be a function of the conflicting goals within the NPR. How can the federal government improve customer service while downsizing a significant portion of the work force? Miller (1994) and Thompson and Jones (1995) believe that NPR's preoccupation with savings may in the long run hinder cultural improvement.

In only one agency did employees perceive improved customer quality (Department of Education).   Likewise in the EPA and the Department of Interior employees perceived stronger "teamwork," while there was no observed change in the difference of means test for the "customer service" question.   Department of Interior employees perceived managers to be stronger in leadership and work organization. Future research could explore the effects of teamwork and supervision on customer satisfaction.

Although this book shows that rewards, supervision, leadership and teamwork may explain federal agency culture, there is no evidence to suggest that the NPR has changed the overall culture of the federal cabinet agencies.   In many respects this conclusion supports Dubnick (1994) and Terry's (1994) ideas on change, and the strength of the government bureaucracy.   Clearly there is a need for more research in this area if the NPR effort will continue at the national level.

The data from this book also support the problems that arise in administrative reform and organizational culture change (March and Olson, 1983; Curdra 1993; Spice, 1994; Miller, 1994; Thompson, 1994 and 1996; Carroll, 1995; Ink, 1995; Kettl, 1996; Fox, 1996; and Hart and Hart, 1997).   This literature attributes these problems to the following: (1) reinventing government was characterized by conflicting goals, and an administrative language rooted in "rhetoric and symbolism" (March and Olsen, 1983;   Miller, 1994; Carroll, 1995; Kettl, 1996 and Hart and Hart, 1997).   This book has shown that government cannot bring about "bottom up" cultural change, and at the same time downsize a major segment of the work force.   Such dichotomous goals cannot reinvent organizational culture and build a talented and motivated public service that is already "sullen and resentful" of reform (Caiden, 1991); (2) in spite of Vice President Al Gore's highly visible role in the NPR, the management culture of the federal cabinet agencies has not changed from 1992 to 1996.   Curdra (1993) and Spice (1994) argue that today's public managers must emerge as "leadership visionaries" who are willing to "take risk." Without these actions future reform efforts are destined to fail; (3) without improved systems of accountability and rewards (Shearer, 1994; and Miller, 1994), the goals of the NPR have little chance to succeed. This book has shown that except for two federal agencies the government's system of rewards and accountability did not change in the time series design.

Clearly successful organizational change is dependent on: (1) the ability and foresight of agency managers to communicate the objectives of reform, and (2) the development of reward systems that reinforce change. This book supports the importance of these conditions in order for reinventing government to succeed now and in the future.

APPENDIX A.

U.S. Merit System Protection Board
Merit Principles Survey

U.S. MERIT SYSTEMS PROTECTION BOARD
WASHINGTON, DC 20419

1996 MERIT PRINCIPLES SURVEY

This survey asks for your opinions and experiences on a variety of personnel issues. The questionnaire is divided into the following three sections:

- SECTION I, COMPLETED BY ALL EMPLOYEES, covers a wide range of areas, including your job; the personnel practices in your work group; whistleblowing; and individual and organizational performance.

- SECTION II, COMPLETED BY SUPERVISORS, concerns managing people.

- SECTION III, COMPLETED BY ALL EMPLOYEES, covers individual background information.

You may not have to answer every question in this survey. Instructions will tell you which questions to skip.

MARKING INSTRUCTIONS

- DON'T use ink or ballpoint pens. Use a No. 2 pencil.
- Erase completely and cleanly any answer you wish to change.
- Don't make any stray marks in this booklet.

CORRECT MARK: INCORRECT MARKS:
○●○○   ⊗◔◉⊘

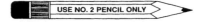
USE NO. 2 PENCIL ONLY

PRIVACY ACT NOTICE

Collection of the requested information is authorized by the Civil Service Reform Act of 1978. Your participation in this survey is completely voluntary and none of the information you choose to supply will be associated with you individually.

REPORT REQUEST ADDRESS

If you would like a copy of the reports published as a result of this survey, please address your request to:

U.S. Merit Systems Protection Board
Office of Policy and Evaluation
1120 Vermont Avenue, NW
Washington, DC 20419

Did you read the marking instructions?
If not, please read them now.

Don't Know/Can't Judge
Strongly Disagree
Disagree
Neither Agree Nor Disagree
Agree
Strongly Agree

1. The work I do on my job is
meaningful to me. .... ○ ○ ○ ○ ○ ○

2. I would recommend the Federal
Government as a place to work. ..... ○ ○ ○ ○ ○ ○

3. I have the skills I need to do my job... ○ ○ ○ ○ ○ ○

4. Overall, I am satisfied with my
current pay. .... ○ ○ ○ ○ ○ ○

5. I need more training to perform my
job effectively. .... ○ ○ ○ ○ ○ ○

6. I have received the training I needed
to keep pace with the requirements
of my job as these have changed. ..... ○ ○ ○ ○ ○ ○

7. In general, I am satisfied with my job.. ○ ○ ○ ○ ○ ○

8. There are too many management
levels in my organization. .... ○ ○ ○ ○ ○ ○

9. I feel my organization is overstaffed
and that it could do the same job
with fewer people if the work
processes could be changed. .... ○ ○ ○ ○ ○ ○

10. The efforts of the National
Performance Review, which has
been working on reinventing
Government, have had a positive
impact in bringing change to
government. .... ○ ○ ○ ○ ○ ○

11. The National Performance Review
has had a positive impact on
improving customer service to
the public. .... ○ ○ ○ ○ ○ ○

12. My organization has made the goals
of the National Performance Review
an important priority. .... ○ ○ ○ ○ ○ ○

13. My organization has made good use
of my knowledge and skills in looking
for ways to become more efficient. .... ○ ○ ○ ○ ○ ○

Don't Know/Can't Judge
Strongly Disagree
Disagree
Neither Agree Nor Disagree
Agree
Strongly Agree

14. My immediate supervisor has good
management skills. .... ○ ○ ○ ○ ○ ○

15. My immediate supervisor has
organized our work group effectively
to get the work done. .... ○ ○ ○ ○ ○ ○

16. Overall, I am satisfied with my
supervisor. .... ○ ○ ○ ○ ○ ○

17. Since the law regarding participation
in partisan political activities by
Federal employees (the Hatch Act)
was changed, I have been more
active in partisan political activities... ○ ○ ○ ○ ○ ○

18. The impact on workforce diversity
should be taken into account when
choosing among best-qualified
candidates. .... ○ ○ ○ ○ ○ ○

19. A spirit of cooperation and teamwork
exists in my immediate work unit..... ○ ○ ○ ○ ○ ○

20. My work unit has a sufficient number
of employees to do its job. .... ○ ○ ○ ○ ○ ○

21. In the past 2 years, the productivity
of my work unit has improved....... ○ ○ ○ ○ ○ ○

22. In the past 2 years, I have been given
more flexibility in how I accomplish
my work. .... ○ ○ ○ ○ ○ ○

23. I am confident that if I lost my Federal
job because of a reduction in force (RIF),
I would be able to find an acceptable
job outside the Federal Government
in a reasonable period of time........ ○ ○ ○ ○ ○ ○

24. The number of people in my work unit
will probably be reduced over the
next 2 years even though our work-
load will stay the same or increase. .. ○ ○ ○ ○ ○ ○

25. The possibility of a reduction in force
(RIF) or furlough has had a negative
effect on my productivity. .... ○ ○ ○ ○ ○ ○

26. My concern about the possibility of
changes in benefits for Federal
employees has had a negative effect
on my productivity. .... ○ ○ ○ ○ ○ ○

Don't Know/Can't Judge
Strongly Disagree
Disagree
Neither Agree Nor Disagree
Agree
Strongly Agree

27. Downsizing has helped my
organization to accomplish its
mission more efficiently. ....○○○○○○

28. A private sector company could
perform the work of my organization
just as effectively as the
Government does. ....○○○○○○

29. Budget cuts have had a negative
effect on my organization's mission
accomplishment. ....○○○○○○

30. Downsizing has seriously eroded
the institutional memory or
knowledge in my organization. ......○○○○○○

31. In general, people of my race/
national origin group are treated
with respect in my organization. .....○○○○○○

32. At the place I work, my opinions
seem to count. ....○○○○○○

33. The work performed by my work unit
provides the public a worthwhile
return on their tax dollars. ....○○○○○○

34. The give and take of public policy-
making doesn't appeal to me. ....○○○○○○

35. Meaningful public service is very
important to me. ....○○○○○○

36. I am not afraid to go to bat for the
rights of others even if it means
I will be ridiculed. ....○○○○○○

37. Making a difference in society
means more to me than personal
achievements. ....○○○○○○

38. I am prepared to make enormous
sacrifices for the good of society. ....○○○○○○

39. I am often reminded by daily events
about how dependent we are on
one another. ....○○○○○○

40. My organization's affirmative employment programs
have frequently resulted in:

Don't Know/Can't Judge
Strongly Disagree
Disagree
Neither Agree Nor Disagree
Agree
Strongly Agree

a. Women being put in positions for
which they were not well-qualified ....○○○○○○
b. Minorities being put in positions for
which they were not well-qualified ....○○○○○○
c. "Reverse" discrimination against
nonminority men ....○○○○○○

41. In the past 2 years, to what extent do you believe you
have been treated fairly regarding the following:

No Basis to Judge
To No Extent
To a Little Extent
To Some Extent
To a Considerable Extent
To a Very Great Extent

a. Promotions ....○○○○○○
b. Awards ....○○○○○○
c. Training ....○○○○○○
d. Annual performance appraisals ......○○○○○○
e. Discipline ....○○○○○○

42. Under Government reinvention initiatives, many new
flexibilities and powers to take employee personnel
actions have been delegated (or may in the future be
delegated) to first-line supervisors. To what extent do
you think your supervisor will exercise the following
authorities in a fair and effective manner:
(Mark a response for each item.)

a. Rating the qualifications of applicants
for jobs ....○○○○○

b. Selecting people for vacancies or
promotions based on their qualifications ..○○○○○

c. Setting individual employees' pay within
broad pay bands ....○○○○○

d. Taking adverse actions such as
suspensions and removals.............○○○○○

43. Have management and the local Federal employee unions established partnerships in your agency?

Yes .... ○
No *(SKIP to question 45)* .... ○
Don't know/Can't judge *(SKIP to question 45)* .... ○

<blockquote>
Don't Know/Can't Judge
To No Extent
To a Minimal Extent
To a Moderate Extent
To a Great Extent
</blockquote>

44. To what extent has the existence of the partnership(s) enabled your organization to better accomplish its mission? .... ○ ○ ○ ○ ○

45. To what extent do you believe that your right to work in an environment that is free from prohibited personnel practices is adequately protected? ...... ○ ○ ○ ○ ○

<blockquote>
No Basis to Judge
Poor
Below average
Average
Above Average
Outstanding
</blockquote>

46. Overall, how would you rate the quality of work performed by:

a. Your current coworkers in your immediate work group .... ○ ○ ○ ○ ○ ○

b. People who have <u>joined</u> your immediate work group from outside the Government in the past 2 years (or since you've been in your work group, if that is less than 2 years) .... ○ ○ ○ ○ ○ ○

c. People who have <u>left</u> the Federal Government from your immediate work group in the last 2 years (or since you've been in your work group, if that is less than 2 years) .... ○ ○ ○ ○ ○ ○

<blockquote>
Don't Know/Can't Judge
No
Yes
</blockquote>

47. <u>In the past 2 years</u>, do you feel you have been denied a job, promotion, or other job benefit because of unlawful discrimination based upon:

a. Race/national origin .... ○ ○ ○
b. Sex .... ○ ○ ○
c. Age .... ○ ○ ○
d. Handicapping condition .... ○ ○ ○
e. Religion .... ○ ○ ○
f. Marital status .... ○ ○ ○
g. Political affiliation .... ○ ○ ○

<blockquote>
Don't Know/Can't Judge
No
Yes
</blockquote>

48. <u>In the past 2 years</u>, do you feel you have been pressured by an agency official:

a. To engage in partisan political activity? .... ○ ○ ○

b. To retaliate against or take an action in favor of another Federal employee or applicant for political reasons? .... ○ ○ ○

49. <u>In the past 2 years</u>, do you feel you have been:

a. Deliberately misled by an agency official about your right to compete for a job or promotion? .... ○ ○ ○

b. Influenced by an agency official to withdraw from competition for a Federal job or promotion in order to help another person's chances for getting that job or promotion? ..... ○ ○ ○

c. Denied a job or promotion because one of the selecting or recommending officials gave an unfair advantage to another applicant? ..... ○ ○ ○

d. Denied a job or promotion which went instead to a relative of one of the selecting or recommending officials? .... ○ ○ ○

50. <u>In the past 2 years</u>, do you feel you have been retaliated against or threatened with retaliation for:

a. Making disclosures concerning health and safety dangers, unlawful behavior, and/or fraud, waste, and abuse? .... ○ ○ ○

b. Exercising any appeal, complaint, or grievance right? .... ○ ○ ○

c. Testifying for or otherwise assisting any individual in the exercise of whistleblowing, equal employment opportunity, or appeal rights? .... ○ ○ ○

d. Refusing to obey an unlawful order? .... ○ ○ ○

e. Reporting unwanted sexual attention or sexual harassment? .... ○ ○ ○

51. (a) If you felt that your rights as a federal employee were violated within the last 2 years, did you take some formal action to try and correct the situation (file a grievance, appeal, etc.)?

Not applicable .... O
Yes .... O
No .... O

(b) If you felt that your rights as a federal employee were violated within the last 2 years and you did *not* take formal action to try and correct this situation, why did you choose not to take any formal action? (mark all that apply)

Not applicable .... O
Still might take some action .... O
Not serious enough .... O
Didn't know I could .... O
Process wouldn't solve the problem .... O
Fear of management retaliation .... O
Problem was resolved informally .... O
Waited too long/missed deadline .... O
Too complicated .... O
Too expensive .... O
Process isn't fair .... O
I left the work unit .... O
Don't know/Can't judge .... O

52. To what extent do you agree with each of the following statements concerning the appeal processes that are available if your organization takes an adverse action against an employee?

                 Don't Know/Can't Judge
                  Strongly Disagree
                   Disagree
           Neither Agree Nor Disagree
                   Agree
                Strongly Agree

a. There are too many different
channels for taking appeals .... O O O O O O

b. The procedures for filing an appeal
are too hard to understand .... O O O O O O

c. The appeal process inappropriately
favors management .... O O O O O O

d. The appeal process inappropriately
favors employees .... O O O O O O

e. The appeal process in my
organization discourages managers
from taking inappropriate actions
against employees .... O O O O O O

f. The appeal process in my
organization keeps supervisors
from taking corrective actions that
should be taken .... O O O O O O

53. In the last 2 years (or since you began working as a Federal civilian employee, if that was less than 2 years ago), did you choose <u>not</u> to apply for any promotion or developmental opportunity (for example, assignment to a high visibility task force) because you felt:

                 Don't Know/Can't Judge
                  No
                 Yes
            Not Applicable

a. you had little or no chance of being
selected because of your race or
national origin? .... O O O O

b. you had little or no chance of being
selected because of your age?............ O O O O

c. you had little or no chance of being
selected because of your sex? .... O O O O

54. How does your pay compare to that of employees outside the Federal Government who are doing jobs similar to yours?

I am paid much less .... O
I am paid somewhat less .... O
I am paid about the same .... O
I am paid somewhat more .... O
I am paid much more .... O
Don't know/Can't judge .... O

55. As a result of budget cuts, downsizing, or reinvention initiatives since 1993, has:

(a) The <u>type</u> of work you perform in your current job changed in a substantial way?

Not applicable .... O
Yes, in a positive manner .... O
Yes, in a negative manner .... O
No .... O
Don't know/Can't judge .... O

(b) The <u>amount</u> of work you perform in your current job changed in a substantial way?

Not applicable .... O
Yes, the amount of work has increased .... O
Yes, the amount of work has decreased .... O
No .... O
Don't know/Can't judge .... O

(c) A change in the location of your job required you to move?

Not applicable .... O
Yes .... O
No .... O
Don't know/Can't judge .... O

56. As a result of possible future budget cuts or downsizing in the next few years, how likely is it that you will:

Don't Know/Can't Judge
Very Unlikely
Somewhat Unlikely
Neither Likely nor Unlikely
Somewhat Likely
Very Likely

a. Voluntarily move to a different job
in your agency? .... ○○○○○○
b. Be required to move to a different job
in your agency under a reduction in
force (RIF)? .... ○○○○○○
c. Move to a different job in the Federal
Government? .... ○○○○○○
d. Leave the Federal Government
voluntarily? .... ○○○○○○
e. Leave the Federal Government
under a reduction in force (RIF)? ..... ○○○○○○
f. Substantially change the type of work
you perform in your current job? ..... ○○○○○○
g. Substantially increase the amount of
work you perform in your current job? ○○○○○○

57. Do you plan to look for another job in the coming year?

No (SKIP to question 60) .... ○
Yes, but only within the Federal Government .... ○
Yes, but only outside of the Federal Government ...... ○
Yes, I plan to look both inside and outside of the
Federal Government .... ○

58. What impact has each of the following had on your decision to look for another job? (If the item does not apply to your situation, please mark "Not applicable.")

Don't Know/Can't Judge
No Impact
Minimal Impact
Moderate Impact
Great Impact
Not Applicable

a. Proposed (or actual) reduction in
force (RIF) .... ○○○○○○
b. Proposed (or actual) furlough .... ○○○○○○
c. Proposed (or actual) demotion,
suspension, firing .... ○○○○○○
d. Reduced opportunity for advancement . ○○○○○○
e. Desire to work in a less stressful
environment .... ○○○○○○
f. Desire for more flexibility in working
conditions (e.g., flexitime, flexiplace,
part-time) .... ○○○○○○
g. Proposed or actual changes in
retirement or other benefits .... ○○○○○○

59. If you are not looking for a job outside of the Government, to what extent did each of the following influence your decision not to seek employment outside the Government?

Don't Know/Can't Judge
To No Extent
To a Minimal Extent
To a Moderate Extent
To a Great Extent
Not Applicable

a. I like working for the Federal
Government .... ○○○○○○
b. I have too much time invested in
the Federal retirement system and
don't want to lose benefits .... ○○○○○○
c. The kind of work I do isn't often
found outside the Government....... ○○○○○○
d. The job market is poor outside the
Government .... ○○○○○○
e. I don't think I could make as much
money outside the Government...... ○○○○○○
f. It is too hard to find out about jobs
outside the Government .... ○○○○○○
g. Employers outside the Government
would not be anxious to hire former
Federal employees................. ○○○○○○

60. Which of the following most closely describes the performance rating you received at your last appraisal?

Outstanding .... ○
Exceeds fully successful .... ○
Fully successful .... ○
Pass .... ○
Minimally successful .... ○
Unacceptable .... ○
Fail .... ○
Have not received a rating .... ○

61. To what extent does your organization accomplish each of the following:

Don't Know/Can't Judge

Less than 70 percent of the time (exceptions occur regularly)

Between 70 and 89 percent of the time
(most of the time, but exceptions are not uncommon)

Between 90 and 99 percent of the time (exceptions are rare)

Always (without exception)

a. Selects well-qualified persons when hiring from outside the agency . . . . ○○○○○

b. Selects persons on the basis of their relative ability, knowledge, and skills when hiring from outside the agency . . . . ○○○○○

c. Promotes people on the basis of their relative ability, knowledge, and skills . . . . ○○○○○

d. Makes selections based on fair and open competition when hiring from outside the agency . . . . ○○○○○

e. Makes selections based on fair and open competition for promotions . . . . ○○○○○

f. Ensures equal pay for equal work . . . . ○○○○○

g. Promotes high standards of integrity, conduct, and concern for the public interest among agency employees . . . . ○○○○○

h. Retains employees on the basis of the adequacy of their performance . . . . ○○○○○

i. Takes appropriate steps to correct inadequate performance . . . . ○○○○○

j. Separates employees who cannot or will not improve their performance to meet required standards . . . . ○○○○○

k. Protects employees against arbitrary personnel actions . . . . ○○○○○

l. Protects employees against personal favoritism . . ○○○○○

m. Protects employees against coercion for partisan political activities . . . . ○○○○○

n. Protects employees against reprisal for whistleblowing . . . . ○○○○○

o. Provides fair and equitable treatment for employees and applicants in all aspects of personnel management without regard to their political affiliation, race, color, religion, national origin, sex, marital status, age, or handicapping condition . . . . ○○○○○

62. Are you a:

Nonsupervisor *(SKIP to Section III, Question 93, Page 12)* . . . . ○

First-level supervisor (i.e., you sign performance appraisals for other employees) . . . . ○

Second or higher-level supervisor or manager . . . ○

SECTION II: SUPERVISORS

63. During the past 2 years, have you supervised employees with poor performance or misconduct problems?

Yes, poor performance . . . . ○

Yes, misconduct . . . . ○

Yes, poor performance and misconduct . . . . ○

No *(Go to question 66)* . . . . ○

Not sure *(Go to question 66)* . . . . ○

64. Which of these problems did you have to deal with most recently?

Poor performance . . . . ○

Misconduct . . . . ○

Mixed (Both) . . . . ○

65. For the problem referred to in question 64, what did you do, and what effect did it have on the employee's behavior?

(Mark ALL that apply, AND where you took an action, mark what effect it had.)

No Basis to Judge

Made Things Worse

Made No Difference

Made Things Better

I took this action:

a. I counseled the employee and worked with him/her informally . . . ○   ○○○○

b. I referred the employee to a counseling service provided by my agency . . . . ○   ○○○○

c. I gave the employee a less-than-satisfactory performance rating . . ○   ○○○○

d. I placed the employee on a Performance Improvement Plan . . ○   ○○○○

e. I initiated formal action against the employee . . . . ○   ○○○○

f. I took no action . . . . ○   ○○○○

g. I have not decided yet what to do . . . . ○   ○○○○

66. Since you have been a Federal supervisor, have you been involved with a complaint or appeal filed by an employee under your supervision with any of the following agencies? (Mark a response for each part of the question.)

	Yes	No	Don't Know
a. Merit Systems Protection Board	○	○	○
b. Office of Personnel Management	○	○	○
c. Equal Employment Opportunity Commission	○	○	○
d. Federal Labor Relations Authority	○	○	○
e. Office of Special Counsel	○	○	○

67. Of these agencies, which one were you involved with most recently?

Merit Systems Protection Board .... ○
Office of Personnel Management .... ○
Equal Employment Opportunity Commission .... ○
Federal Labor Relations Authority .... ○
Office of the Special Counsel .... ○
No involvement with any of these agencies .... ○

68. If you dealt with a complaint or appeal filed with one of the above agencies, regarding the most recent involvement you had, how satisfied were you with the way in which this case was handled?

Not applicable .... ○
Very satisfied .... ○
Somewhat satisfied .... ○
Neither satisfied nor dissatisfied .... ○
Somewhat dissatisfied .... ○
Very dissatisfied .... ○
Don't know/Can't judge .... ○

69. In the past 3 years, has the quality of applicants for vacancies in your work group improved or worsened, with regard to EACH of the following categories of positions?

Don't Know/Can't Judge
Greatly Worsened
Somewhat Worsened
Remained the Same
Somewhat Improved
Greatly Improved
No Basis to Judge
(e.g., had no vacancies to fill)

a. Wage Grade (trades and crafts)	○	○	○	○	○	○
b. Clerical or support	○	○	○	○	○	○
c. Technical (e.g., engineering, biological or medical technician or aide)	○	○	○	○	○	○
d. Entry-level professional or administrative positions	○	○	○	○	○	○
e. Mid- or senior-level professional or administrative positions	○	○	○	○	○	○
f. Senior Executive Service (SES)	○	○	○	○	○	○

Don't Know/Can't Judge
Strongly Disagree
Disagree
Neither Agree Nor Disagree
Agree
Strongly Agree

70. Since 1993, I have gained additional flexibility in taking personnel actions. ○ ○ ○ ○ ○ ○

71. I am held accountable for the level of representation of minorities and women in my work unit. ○ ○ ○ ○ ○ ○

72. I am held accountable for the level of representation of persons with disabilities in my work unit. ○ ○ ○ ○ ○ ○

73. In the last two years, I had the opportunity to take actions which could affect the level of representation of minorities, women, or persons with disabilities, in my work unit. ○ ○ ○ ○ ○ ○

Don't Know/Can't Judge
Strongly Disagree
Disagree
Neither Agree Nor Disagree
Agree
Strongly Agree
Not applicable, never received such training

74. Training I have received in managing diversity has helped me to be a better supervisor. ○ ○ ○ ○ ○ ○ ○

75. Since the Government undertook its recent efforts to downsize, there has been a noticeable reduction in the number of supervisory positions in my organization. ○ ○ ○ ○ ○ ○

76. Which of the following groups, if any, do you think will be the most adversely affected by any efforts your organization takes in the near future to reduce the number of supervisors and managers?

Minorities .... ○
Women .... ○
Nonminority men .... ○
Minorities and women equally .... ○
Each group equally without regard to sex or race/national origin .... ○
Don't know .... ○

77. **How long have you been a supervisor?**

Less than 1 year *(SKIP to question 80)* .... ○
1-2 years *(SKIP to question 80)* .... ○
3-5 years .... ○
More than 5 years .... ○

78. **How have your responsibilities as a supervisor/ manager changed over the last 2 years?**

Increased greatly .... ○
Increased somewhat .... ○
Stayed the same .... ○
Decreased somewhat .... ○
Decreased greatly .... ○
Don't know/Can't judge .... ○

79. **How has the number of employees you supervise changed in the last 2 years?**

Increased greatly .... ○
Increased slightly .... ○
Stayed the same .... ○
Decreased slightly .... ○
Decreased greatly .... ○
Don't know/Can't judge .... ○

80. **The Office of Personnel Management is responsible for assuring that Federal personnel management is implemented consistent with the merit system principles concerning fair and equitable treatment. To what extent do you believe OPM is effective in assuring that agency personnel actions are consistent with the merit system principles?**

To a great extent .... ○
To a moderate extent .... ○
To a minimal extent .... ○
To no extent .... ○
Don't know/Can't judge .... ○
Not aware of such an OPM effort .... ○

81. **To your knowledge, has your personnel office experienced any downsizing?**

Yes .... ○
No *(SKIP to question 83)* .... ○
Don't know/Can't judge *(SKIP to question 83)* .... ○

82. **Below are listed possible outcomes of downsizing personnel office staffs. Please mark the outcome that you believe describes the results of downsizing in the personnel office staff that services your unit. Since the personnel office downsizing:**

a. **The speed of processing actions has**

Not applicable; haven't downsized or
  haven't needed them since downsizing .... ○
Improved .... ○
Gotten worse .... ○
Not changed; still fast .... ○
Not changed; still slow .... ○
Not changed; still acceptable .... ○
Don't know/Can't judge .... ○

b. **The availability of staff to assist me has**

Not applicable; haven't downsized or
  haven't needed them since downsizing .... ○
Improved .... ○
Gotten worse .... ○
Not changed; still readily available .... ○
Not changed; still not readily available .... ○
Not changed; still reasonably available .... ○
Don't know/Can't judge .... ○

c. **The quality of assistance provided by personnel has**

Not applicable; haven't downsized or
  haven't needed them since downsizing .... ○
Improved .... ○
Gotten worse .... ○
Not changed; still high quality .... ○
Not changed; still poor quality .... ○
Not changed; still acceptable .... ○
Don't know/Can't judge .... ○

83. **To what extent do you believe you typically need assistance from your personnel office when you take the following kinds of personnel actions?**

Don't Know/Can't Judge
To No Extent
To a Minimal Extent
To a Moderate Extent
To a Great Extent

a. Recruiting applicants .... ○○○○○
b. Evaluating candidates for a vacancy .... ○○○○○
c. Hiring a new employee .... ○○○○○
d. Classifying a job .... ○○○○○
e. Determining performance awards ...... ○○○○○
f. Suspending, demoting, or removing
  a subordinate employee .... ○○○○○
g. Developing training plans for your
  employees .... ○○○○○

84. To what extent do you personally feel prepared to take on greater responsibility in each of the following areas?

Don't Know/Can't Judge
To No Extent
To a Minimal Extent
To a Moderate Extent
To a Great Extent

a. Recruiting applicants . . . . ○○○○○

b. Evaluating candidates for a vacancy . . . . ○○○○○

c. Hiring an employee . . . . ○○○○○

d. Classifying a job . . . . ○○○○○

e. Determining performance awards . . . . . . ○○○○○

f. Suspending, demoting, or removing
a subordinate employee . . . . ○○○○○

g. Developing training plans for your
employees . . . . ○○○○○

85. Have you hired anyone in the last 2 years?
Yes . . . . ○
No *(SKIP to question 88)* . . . . ○

86. Were you given candidates to consider under a priority placement system?
Yes . . . . ○
No *(SKIP to question 88)* . . . . ○
Don't know/Can't judge . . . . ○

87. How did these candidates compare to candidates not in the priority placement system?
Not applicable . . . . ○
Much better . . . . ○
Somewhat better . . . . ○
Neither better nor worse . . . . ○
Somewhat worse . . . . ○
Much worse . . . . ○
Don't know/Can't judge . . . . ○

88. To what extent are you confident that you could select a well-qualified person for a vacancy if you were required to give priority consideration to displaced employees from other agencies?
Not applicable; all of my positions are so unique
that no other agency would have employees
who could qualify for them . . . . ○
To a great extent . . . . ○
To a moderate extent . . . . ○
To a minimal extent . . . . ○
To no extent . . . . ○
Don't know/Can't judge . . . . ○

89. To what extent have budget cuts hindered your ability to hire the best qualified candidates (e.g., because there were insufficient funds to move candidates to a new location)?
Not applicable . . . . ○
To a great extent . . . . ○
To a moderate extent . . . . ○
To a minimal extent . . . . ○
To no extent . . . . ○
Don't know/Can't judge . . . . ○

90. What effect do you believe that classifying jobs into a reduced number of broad bands incorporating several grade levels instead of using the current 15 General Schedule grade levels (with increased flexibility in setting pay rates) would have on your ability to hire qualified job applicants?
Very positive effect . . . . ○
Somewhat positive effect . . . . ○
Neither positive nor negative effect . . . . ○
Somewhat negative effect . . . . ○
Very negative effect . . . . ○
Don't know/Can't judge . . . . ○

91. In the last 2 years, have you avoided taking an adverse action against an employee that you thought might have been warranted?
Yes . . . . ○
No *(SKIP to question 93)* . . . . ○
Don't know/Can't judge *(SKIP to question 93)* . . . . ○

92. Please rate the extent to which each of the following affected your decision not to take the adverse action.

Don't Know/Can't Judge
To No Extent
To a Minimal Extent
To a Moderate Extent
To a Great Extent

a. Concern about cost to agency if
employee appealed . . . . ○○○○○
b. Concern about time required to take
such an action (including possible
appeals) . . . . ○○○○○
c. Concern about the effect taking the
action would have on the entire work
group . . . . ○○○○○
d. Lack of familiarity with procedures for
taking such an action . . . . ○○○○○
e. Concern about possibility employee
would file an EEO complaint . . . . ○○○○○
f. Concern that upper-level management
would not support my action . . . . ○○○○○
g. Other (please briefly explain in
comments section) . . . . ○○○○○

SECTION III: ALL EMPLOYEES

93. How many years have you been a Federal Government employee (excluding military service)?

Less than 1 year ... ○	16 to 20 years ..... ○
1 to 5 years .... ○	21 to 25 years ..... ○
6 to 10 years ...... ○	26 to 30 years ..... ○
11 to 15 years ..... ○	31 years or more ... ○

94. How many years have you been in your current position?

Less than 1 year ... ○	4 to 10 years ...... ○
1 to 3 years .... ○	More than 10 years . ○

95. Are you:

Male .... ○   Female .... ○

96. What is your age?

Under 20 .... ○	50 - 54 .... ○
20 - 29 .... ○	55 - 59 .... ○
30 - 39 .... ○	60 - 64 .... ○
40 - 49 .... ○	65 or older .... ○

97. What is your highest educational level?

Less than high school diploma .... ○
High school diploma or GED .... ○
High school diploma or GED plus some college
    or technical school .... ○
2-year college degree (AA, AS) .... ○
4-year college degree (BA, BS, or other bachelor's
    degree)...................................... ○
Some graduate or professional school .... ○
Graduate or professional degree .... ○

98. What is your pay category?

General schedule (GS/GM) or similar .... ○
Wage grade .... ○
Executive (SES or equivalent).................... ○
Other .... ○

99. What is your current pay grade?

1 ..... ○	7 .. ○	13 .... ○
2 ..... ○	8 .. ○	14 .... ○
3 ..... ○	9 .. ○	15 .... ○
4 ..... ○	10 .. ○	ES-1 – ES-6
5 ..... ○	11 .. ○	(SES pay grades).. ○
6 ..... ○	12 .. ○	Other .... ○

100. Do you work at your agency's headquarters office (typically in Washington, DC), or in a field location?

Headquarters ...... ○   Field location ...... ○

101. Is your immediate supervisor:

General schedule (GS/GM) .... ○
Wage grade (WS) .... ○
Military .... ○
SES .... ○
Other .... ○

102. Are you:

African American (not of Hispanic origin) .... ○
Asian Pacific American .... ○
Hispanic .... ○
Native American .... ○
White (not of Hispanic origin) .... ○
Other .... ○

103. Where do you work?

Agriculture .... ○
Commerce .... ○
Defense
    Air Force .... ○
    Army... ○
    Navy... ○
    Other DOD.................................... ○
Education .... ○
Energy .... ○
Environmental Protection Agency .... ○
General Services Administration .... ○
Health and Human Services .... ○
Housing and Urban Development .... ○
Justice .... ○
Labor .... ○
Interior .... ○
National Aeronautics and Space Administration ..... ○
Office of Personnel Management .... ○
Small Business Administration .... ○
Social Security Administration .... ○
State .... ○
Transportation .... ○
Treasury .... ○
Veterans Affairs .... ○
Other .... ○

```
COMMENTS: (Enclose extra sheets if needed)
_____
_____
_____
_____
_____
_____
_____
_____
_____
```

Please seal the questionnaire in the prepaid envelope and return it to the private contractor below who is processing the results. Thank you for your assistance.

RESEARCH APPLICATIONS, INC.
414 Hungerford Drive, Suite 210
Rockville, MD 20850-4125
ATTN: MSPB-MPS4

APPENDIX B.
FOCUS INTERVIEWS

Focus Interviews with four members of the NPR Staff
March 13, 1997

Question (Nufrio): Reinventing government and NPR appears to be
a management approach based on principles that attempt to change the
culture of government... one of the principles is to drive decision
making down to the lowest employee level... freeing employees, in the
Vice President's words in NPR I... to becomes thinkers and doers...
where do you see decision making driven down to the lowest employee
level ?

Answer (NPR Staff): I think HUD (Housing and Urban Development)
has driven decision making down through a significant reduction in
management positions... and a matter of fact... all of their regional
director positions I believe were deleted thus removing a level in the
hierarchy in cases where it didn't add value. HUD has done a
tremendous job in responding to the President's call to reduce its
headquarters positions by 50 percent and their multi-family housing
directors.

They are currently now involved in a re-engineering project to
change the way they do business altogether. I think HUD is an agency
that is moving in the right direction.

Question (Nufrio): How about the organizational structure as it relates
to decision making. Have you noticed any agencies changes to the
organizational structure which affected decision making?

Answer (NPR Staff): The HUD example is a good one... Because of
the elimination of regional officers... I think that you have seen at the
office of Personal management a major reduction in staff... having an
impact on the organizational structure... there are certain functions that
they had early in administration that they no longer have... OPM also
privatized the whole investigations operation and turned it into an
Employee Stock Ownership Plan (ESOP).

Question (Nufrio): Any other agencies where you notice a change in
the structure of the organization?

Answer (NPR Staff): When I say a change in the structure, I can't say that this speaks particularly to taking a function (a major function that was in the organization) and now privatizing it out in terms of whether they changed the command or whatever, I can't speak for them. I do know that HUD eliminated the whole level of the regional office.

Question (Nufrio): When the NPR started, the Vice President was very visible... cheerleading the principles of NPR to the federal agencies... and to me that represents the kind of visible leadership that needs to take place in a major change effort of this kind. Have you noticed any agencies where that same visible leadership is working?

Answer (NPR Staff): I think Susan mentioned that James Whitt at FEMA, made some significant changes that they made in terms of reinventing their organization if the direction had not been sent from the top.

HUD Secretary Andrew Cuomo just received the JFK Kennedy school Award for innovation last year for their program and he has a real philosophy of reinvention innovation. So I think that will continue with HUD.

Another organization is the Social Security Administration... their efforts customer service... But you know, these are only a few examples and right now we are going around to the 21 agencies that have the most customers and really asking the agency heads to step up to the plate.

Question (Nufrio): And what kind of responses are you getting from the leadership of those agencies to that charge? Are there any agencies that are saying that they will be more proactive in the next three years?

NPR Staff: The Vice President is asking that reinvention be the core part of their strategic business plan by September... so yes he... is asking for 4 year commitments and to make customer service an important part.

When we talk about customer service, agencies that have made the most significant improvement in customer service... since we started back in 1993 with maybe less than 10 customer service standards... to having customer service standards to somewhere around the thousands today.

Question (Nufrio): Now one of the recommendations in NPR I was to provide adequate training, and upgrade employees with information technology skills, and narrow the restrictions on employee training. Along the lines of noticing any change in the skills and knowledge of the federal work... looking at this whole area of training... are there any agencies which have invested more than others?

Answer (NPR staff): James Whit of FEMA has trained every employee in customer service in his agency... so I think that is a great example.

Nufrio: So every employee was trained in customer service?

Answer (NPR staff): I think it's customer service but I think goes beyond customer service... where you talk about reinventing an agency where training becomes an integral part of it, it's not so much that it's something unique. Most of our federal agencies are looking at not just doing training for training sake, but they are targeting to the core functions and core skills that they need to take their organizations into the next millennium.

Nufrio: Any other agencies which stand out in this area?

Answer (NPR staff): HHS (Health and Human Services). Donna Shalala has actually signed a multi page document showing the investment in the work force in that organization is important... making a commitment as to how the human resources of HHS would be the integral foundation for taking HHS into the future... and her commitment to them personally in the area of enhancing... not only work life but their personal lives in support of both lives, the training that is required, etc... major culture change in an organization, a large organization and especially coming from the top.

Nufrio: Participatory management was one of the Osborne and Gaebler tenents to "reinventing government"... to quote Osborne and Gaebler, "the reinventing manager must use participatory management to accomplish the goals of reinvention." Was this made a part of the NPR process and program... participatory management?

Answer (NPR): I would not call it the Osborne and Gaebler model, but a model that the Vice President took from the private sector.

We have also had a real push to eliminate the personal supervisory jobs in regard to team leaders and we have a lot of self employed work teams emerging... I think your best example is the President and Vice President themselves... you see them participating in the leadership in this administration and the leadership of our federal government... last year, the President and the Vice President were at a symposium at Georgetown University with senior businessmen who were responsible for having the best organizations that supported work family life cultures... to me, that's a real commitment from the top in terms of what types of work force and work force environment they want to have... when we talk about people like James Whit... whenever there is a disaster, you don't see him sitting behind a desk talking about it...

you see him out there at the site talking to the people there, with his employers... with his shirt sleeves rolled up and working... and I think that starts at the top and we are seeing it.

There is also a directive in HHS by Donna Shalala set by February to get rid of time sheets... They are going to eliminate time sheets because time sheets instill a culture of distrust... As a professional employee and you are going to be there all day... but, signing in and signing out. . is a system where time is managed, not work... and what Donna Shalala is trying to get at is that job evaluations are based managing work, not the time... people are responsible for getting the job done... this is a big cultural transformation.

Nufrio: What about the self-managed work teams?

NPR Staff: Now with self managed work teams you have to realize that the cultural transformation takes about five years... so what we're seeing now is the front end where former supervisors are now team leaders... And so some of those supervisors are still acting like supervisors... but, you know, that historical perceptive is going to fade and you know the change is going to happen... Joe Thompson, the head of the VA benefit office in New York, is a great example of something where changes in going to self-managed work teams is taking place.

Nufrio: Who drove the concept of that in SSA? Who was most responsible for it?

NPR Staff: I would say that Jay Schraeder, the head of the Social Security Commission ... , and you see, now, you have to remember that this is still getting negative publicity... People are saying, "wow, they are still acting like supervisors," but you know you're looking at the front end of a transformation, not the back end.

I think one of the best examples is right here at NPR... we practice what we preach... this is a very flat organization, we're a self directed work team, and that's unique because the people that make up the staff here are representative of federal agencies across the United States ... and they come out of an environment where there may be a very hierarchal structure ... and they come here and have an opportunity to work in this total flat organization ... we're learning ourselves as we go along, about the uniqueness of it... you know, if there's Xeroxing to do, you do your own Xeroxing .. . If someone needs help and you're in power to make sure that person's served and give them their help ... . And then with our director here, all he wants to know is that you've done a good job.

Nufrio: I just have a few more questions ...   National Partnership

Councils ... Again, one of the goals of the 1993 report was to encourage these labor management partnerships, which is a form of encouraging participation. . .. what have you noticed in this area in terms of observed change?

NPR Staff: I think that the agencies have done a good job, but there is still a lot of work to do. I think that to date we have somewhere in the neighborhood of about 800 partnerships, which is tremendous... in fact we have some agencies that have received awards for their endeavors in the way that they used the partnership to enhance the delivery of their services ... as well as reduce cost, such as the U.S. Mint.

I think that there are some agencies that aren't real sure yet how to do partnerships. As a result of that, the National Partnership Council for the first time since its formation has decided to work with challenged partnerships ... They will try to mentor partnerships that are having some difficulty learning about partnerships ... and that's just an admirable task for an elected body, because many times when you're on a forum such as this, people just come together and talk. These members have decided they actually want to sit down with management and labor where there are challenged partnerships and see what they can do to facilitate success. We're just starting that process and we're real excited about that. I think that what's going on in the Federal Government in the area of partnership is new .. . I think there is still some growing pains.

It's interesting that, when the NPR was first formed, and the vice president was listening to business leaders... one of the things that they said was very important was establishing partnerships with our labor unions. And as a result of that, we've done some work in four years ... Now we are going back to some of those people who suggested that, just to kind of see what they're doing differently.

I'd like to give you an idea ... an example of how it's working every day here too .. . I don't know if you read the newspaper yesterday about the president's radio speech, radio address about welfare to work ... Even though the Federal Government is downsizing ... he says we're still the largest employer and that we are going to help with the welfare to work mission... Which means the federal government is going to stand up to the plate and help hire people coming off welfare rolls... Well, before, while he was making that announcement, our boss, was visiting the head of AFGE in the hospital ... to make sure that the union is on board... And they came to some agreement about how this would be done and I think that's really remarkable so that they are being consulted at the front end of a major policy change that would affect employees .. .   So we're living it, like she said about the way our environment is set up .. .   The vice president's office is the living partnership, dealing with it initially.

Nufrio: Of the 800 partnerships that exist, are there any agencies leading the class on that?

NPR Staff: I think she mentioned the U.S. Mint.
DOD has won some awards.. . The IRS has won some awards.

Nufrio: Any DOD agencies, like Army, Navy, that stand out?

NPR Staff: It's interesting, DOD has formed their own partnership so they are working in partnership with all the other unions and as a result .. that endeavor was saluted by the National Partnership Council ... and some of their specific entities have been cited.

Nufrio: Developing rewards and   incentive systems... making government more customer oriented. .. Holding employees accountable. Are there any agencies that have stepped up accountability?

One complaint about accountability is that agencies ... up to this point have measured what they can measure ... and what they've measured for individual employees often hasn't been what we wanted to measure ... especially for regulatory agencies.

What they ended up measuring were things like ... the number of fines levied ... the number of citations given, not results. Our biggest change is to try to get agencies to measure results. Again, OSHA has done some great things with reducing worker accident rates as a measure of success... not the number of fines levied or citations given. This is what the whole government performance results act speaks to ... getting the federal government to measure actual results...   So for Social Security, we say they are getting performance results when the private sector decided to give them an award for the 800 system.. . But oftentimes the performance measures used in government do not measure performance. As a matter of fact I did a study of regulatory agencies a few years ago and I found... in about fifty agencies ... 20 percent of the measures had something to do with cooperation, communication and success. Most of them were all 'got you' and process measures... such as 'I turned in my reports on time... I dressed right'... All kinds of goofy stuff and it didn't speak to performance.

Nufrio: When you think about personnel administration, in the past it's always been so much dictated by--are you adhering to this rule?... Are you adhering to this regulation?

NPR Staff: ... If there is one group of people that are facing reinvention, those are the people who work in human resources. They either have to move from being technical specialists of laws to being consultants and advisors to managers in order to help them get the work force that they need to get the job accomplished... so we're working with those groups to understand the importance of the outcome, not necessarily the input, the outcome and what's your result?

Your result is to have the right place, the right worker with the right tools in the right place ... and the way you get that is by working with your managers and partnership not necessarily saying you can't do this... and the rule says this and the rule says that. And we're working to attempt to reinvent here in human resources through the use of our performance based organizations.

That's a new concept that we have borrowed from Britain, they call it their next step agency and we're using it to give our federal agencies... a lot of flexibility in being able to achieve their goals by having some flexibility in the HR area... having some flexibility in procurement, but the greatest flexibility is being able to put a person at the top of that particular organization who is not necessarily a federal worker..., but is someone who has demonstrated expertise in the private sector... is under contract... if they don't perform, then they will be out.

You have to look at human resources. You mentioned you've been to Merit Systems Protection Board. Are you are working with MSPD? I think it's real important for you to talk to them about the culture of personnel in the government... It's my understanding that, correct me if I'm wrong, that in terms of federal government, most of the upward mobility, one of the greatest areas of upward mobility has been the human resources area... People came in at entry level jobs and have moved up with on the job training and assumption of duties. If you're now looking to affect a culture change using these people as the heart of your culture... I think one issue is how to get these people, who grew up in an agency, to see this is the way we've always done it... to be the people on the forefront of change... what do you think about it?

And also, the fact that you're going see less of them. Many of your personnel functions are being regionalized so you won't have individual offices here, there and every where... So we are going to see a lot of those individuals downsized or no longer in those jobs... so at the same time, we're reducing the number of people who do that work and then also asking them that they need to change the way they do it because it won't be the way it used to be.

Nufrio: Other than OSHA, any other agencies that kind of stand out in class with respect to accountability and performance systems?

NPR Staff: Well I think, I'm not sure how that's translated to performance, but I do know that Agriculture is moving really hard in that area and I think AMS (Agriculture Marketing Service) was the first agency that I am aware of that had actual performance plans, with customer input... The Department of Education is working with 360 degree performance plan.

Nufrio: And how long have they had that in place?

NPR Staff: They used it on a trial basis for about a year. It's been less than a year that it's been department wide, and the senior executives, they're only a two level system, either satisfactory or unsatisfactory.

Nufrio: Any other agencies, other than education and agriculture?

NPR Staff: Keep in mind that this is an area that has been decentralized... so agencies are not required to let us know what they are doing. We just have to be assured that whatever they are doing will support systems when it comes to reduction in force or whatever, so I'd say there are probably quite a few agencies out there doing it..., but since we decentralized that back to the agencies.

Nufrio: OK rewards and incentive systems, the intent was that again reinventing government, making government more customer oriented through incentive systems.   Have you noticed any agencies where they've reinvented their incentive systems?

NPR Staff: DOL, I think, and Education, like you said... the '360' performance evaluation... now the customers are actually part of that employee's evaluation... We've been encouraging secretarial awards in various kinds of reinforcement and reinvention efforts...   Just this morning the Vice President gave an award at the National League of Cities to OSHA and the City of Scotsdale for their partnership... Another Vice President's award is going to Peace Corps for putting their recruitment system on the net... You know, applications are up, people kind of access them to the Website.

Nufrio: When we talked about last week... you said that in looking at data by agency... wasn't really telling you much... but that in terms of the overall results... you have found that there are 'islands of excellence' that have emerged from NPR?

NPR Staff: Well, what I think I said was that I didn't think you'd find it in culture surveys... that things could change drastically because what we're seeing is that the various agencies are good at various things... like HHS has eliminated time sheets... that would be an island of excellence... An island of excellence might be Department of State ... the Bureau of Counselor Affairs Website where you can apply for passport... get the application for a passport online... or you can get Social Security to come back and give you your estimate of earnings by doing it online... There are islands of excellence all through the government. We know what reinvention looks like because a lot of agencies have done pieces of it. What we don't know is whether agencies are completely transformed... FEMA is far along... HUD is far along... But what we don't have is a situation where we can look at an agency and say, boy, you know, this has agency done everything.

Interview With Merit Systems Protection Board Staff

Nufrio: Are you somewhat familiar with the MSPB survey in 1992... when comparing it to 1996 do you notice any changes in the survey results?

MSPB Answer: There are some patterns that emerge as it relates to NPR items. When we would look at the relationship of those items to other questions... for example when people say that they see NPR as a priority... we correlated the NPR question with other questions... there is a significant correlation with some of these questions.

Nufrio: Was there an actual shift in the responses by question from 1992 to 1996?

MSPB Staff: We look at the actual responses... and create a binomial profile..., for example the total number of employees who agree with job satisfaction, did that go up or down... There was not a big change with job satisfaction...

the cooperation question has gone up a little bit.

Nufrio: The question, "supervisor has leadership skills", did that shift at all?

MSPB: It didn't change that much

Nufrio: How about on the awards/rewards system question?

MSPB : There is a slight improvement... there are many ways to slice the data.

Getting back to NPR we noticed a correlation in this area... the same with downsizing... some will say downsizing was caused by NPR... Actually when we look at downsizing and compare the correlations of that question to the culture variables... the effect is not as strong as NPR... what it is saying is that downsizing has occurred, but it doesn't have the same effect as NPR.

Nufrio: What is your measure of downsizing?

MSPB: It is whether "downsizing has helped my organization? People will say basically no to that... on the other hand we know that downsizing has occurred... downsizing has definitely had an effect but it is not as strong as I would have thought.

Nufrio: How about the employee skills question?**MSPB:** That one has remained the same as in 1992... most of these questions we get very little change...   The downsizing question typically goes up in some administration's and then levels off.

Nufrio: But you never really look at change in survey questions at the agency level?

MSPB: That is right... the sample is not large enough to look at agencies.

Nufrio: Any thing else in terms of the shifts in the questions?

MSPB: I have not really looked at it in great detail to answer that... I have seen very little shifts... the interesting factor was the patterns of responses, what items correlate with each others... we are in a sense trying to hypothesize what items relate to others... that is NPR seen as a goal within the agency... the levels of management being reduced, etc.

Endnotes

[1] The total savings is derived from three sources. First, $73.4 billion in savings from implementing the recommendations of NPRI. Second, $24 billion in savings from additional recommendations in NPRII. And third, more than $21.5 billion in savings from agency reinvention efforts beyond the recommendation of NPR I and II. (Gore 1996,1)

[2] *.05 level of significance
 **.01 level of significance
***.005 level of significance

[3] There is a negative or positive category for each cultural question by agency. A negative means that employees agree less on the cultural question (at a level of significance) than in 1992. A positive means that there is greater agreement.

REFERENCES

Adams, Thomas. "Military Doctrine and the Organization Culture of the United States Army." Ph.D. diss., Syracuse University, 1991.

Argyris, Chris. "Organizational Man: Rational and Self-Rationalizing." *Public Administration Review* 33 (1973): 354-357.

Argyris, Chris. *Organizational Learning.* Reading MA: Addison-Wesley, 1993.

Argyris, Chris. *Reasoning, Learning and Action.* San Francisco: Jossey-Bass, 1982.

Argyris, Chris. "Some Limits of Rational Man Organizational Theory." *Public Administration Review* 33 (1973): 253-267.

Arnold, John E., and Barry Selberg. "Mastering The Practical Politics of Getting Your Ideas Adopted." *Governing.* June, 1991. 10

Arnold, Peri E. *Making the Managerial Presidency.* Princeton, New Jersey: Princeton University Press, 1986.

Arnold, Peri E. "Reform's Changing Role." *Public Administration Review* 55 (1995): 407-417.

Balk, Walter L., Geert Bouckaert, and Kevin M. Bronner. "Notes on the Theory and Practice of Government Productivity Improvement." *Public Productivity Review* 8 (1989): 399-413

Ban, Carolyn, and Norma Riccucci. "Personnel Systems and Labor Relations: Steps Toward a Quiet Revitalization." In *Revitalizing State and Local Public Service.* edited by Frank J. Thompson. San Francisco: Jossey-Bass, 1993. 71-103.

Barnard, Chester I., *Functions of the Executive.* Cambridge, MA: Harvard University Press, 1938.

Barr, Stephen. "Gore Sees Cynicism Endangering Reform." *Washington Post* 14, July 1994. Sec A.

Bate, P. "The Impact of Organizational Culture on Approaches to Organizational-Problem Solving." *Organizational Studies* 5 (1984): 43-66.

Bellavita, Christopher. "Heros, Not Leaders." *The Bureaucrat* Winter, 1989-1990: 12.

Benedict, R. *Patterns of Culture.* New York: Houghton-Mifflin, 1934.

Benne, Kenneth. *The Discipline of Practical Judgement in a Democratic Society.* Chicago: University of Chicago Press, 1943.

Benne Kenneth, Leland P. Bradford, Jack R. Gibb, and Ronald O. Lippitt. *The Laboratory Method of Changing and Learning: Theory and Application.* Palo Alto, Ca.: Science and Behavior Books, 1975.

Bennis, Warren. *Changing Organizations.* New York: Jossey-Bass, 1966.

Bennis, Warren. *Beyond Bureaucracy.* New York: McGraw-Hill, 1973

Bennis, Warren. *Beyond Bureaucracy, Essays on the Development and Evolution of Human Organization.* San Francisco: Jossey-Bass, 1993.

Biggerstaff, Charlotte. 1990. "Creating, Managing and Transforming Organizational Culture in the Community College". Ph.D. diss., The University of Texas, 1990.

Billesbach, T., and M. Schniederjans. "Applicability of Just-In-Time Techniques in Administration." *Production and Inventory Management* 30 (1989): 40-44.

Blau, Peter. *The Dynamics of Bureaucracy.* Chicago: University of Chicago Press, 1955.

Boshoff, Christo, and Gerhard Mels. "A Causal Model to Evaluate the Relationships among Supervision, Role Stress, Organizational Commitment and Internal Service Quality." *European Journal of Marketing.* 29 (1995): 23-42.

Brady F. Neil, and Gary Woller. "The 'Ideal' and the 'Real' in Administrative Ethics." Presented at 1994 National American Political Science Association Conference. New York.

Bryman, Alan. "The Debate About Quantitative and Qualitative Research: A Question of Method or Epistemology." *The British Journal of Sociology* 35 (1984).

Caiden, Gerald E. *Administrative Reform Comes of Age.* New York: Berlin, 1991.

Carroll, James D. "The Rhetoric of Reform and Political Reality in the National Performance Review." *Public Administration Review* 55 (1995): 302-312.

Chatman, Jennifer A., and Karen A. Jehn. "Assessing the Relationship Between Industry Characteristics and Organizational Culture." *Academy of Management Journal* 37 (1994): 522-553.

Cleveland, Harlan. *The Knowledge Executive.* New York: E.P. Dutton, 1985.

Commission on Economy and Efficiency. *The Need for A National Budget.* Washington, D.C.: GPO, 1912.

Conant, James K. "In the Shadow of Wilson and Brownlow: Executive Branch Reorganization in the States, 1965 to 1987." *Public Administration Review*(1988): 892-898.

Covey, S.R. *Principle-CenteredLeadership.* New York: Summit Books, 1991.

Curda, Elizabeth H. "Reinventing Government: Moving Beyond the Buzzwords." *Public Manager* 22 (1993): 33-36.

Datta, Lois-Ellen. "Strange Bedfellows: The Politics of Qualitative Methods." *American Behavioral Scientist* 26 (1992): 133-144.

Davenport-Sypher, B., Applegate, J.L. and Sypher, H.E., "Culture and Communication in Organizational Contexts." In *Communication, Culture, and Organizational Processes.* Edited by W.B. Gudykunst, L.P. Stewart, and S. Ting-Toomey. Beverly Hills, CA: Sage Publications, 1985.

Davy, Jeanette, A., Richard E. White, Nancy J. Merrit, and Karen Grtizmacher. "A Deprivation of the Underlying Constructs of Just-In-Time Management Systems." *Academy of Management Journal* 35 (1992): 653-670.

Denhardt, Robert B. *In the Shadow of Organization.* Lawrence, KA: University of Kansas Press, 1981.

Downs, G.W., and L. B. Mohr. "Conceptual Issues In the Study of Innovation." *Administrative Science Quarterly* 21 (1976): 700-714.

Dubnick, Melvin J. "A Coup Against King Bureaucracy." In *Deregulating The Public Service; Can Government Be Improved.* Edited by John DiIulio. Washington, D.C.: Brookings Institution, 1994.

Drucker, Peter. *The Age of Discontinuity.* New York: Harper Torchbooks, 1968.

Dwyer Paula, Peter Engardio, Zachary Schiller, and Stanley Reed. "Tearing Up Today's Organization Chart." *Fortune.* May,1995: 80.

Dyer, W.G. "The Cycle of Cultural Evolution in Organizations." In *Gaining Control of the Corporate Culture* Edited by R.H. Kilman, M.J. Saxton and R. Serpa. San Francisco, CA: Jossey-Bass, 1985.

Epstein Paul D. "Measuring and Analyzing the Productivity of Professionals and Managers," In *Public Productivity Handbook.* Edited by Marc Holzer. New York: Marcel Dekker, 1992.

Epstein, Paul, D. E. Greenberg, and M. J. Thier. "Improving Productivity of Professionals and Managers." In *Public Productivity Handbook.* Edited by Marc Holzer. New York: Marcel Dekker, 1992.

Fayol, Henri. *General and Industrial Management.* London: Pitman, 1949.

Federal Quality Institute. *U.S. Tank-Automotive Research, Development and Engineering Center.* Washington, DC: Federal Quality Institute, 1994.

Follett, Mary Parker. *Creative Experience and Dynamic Administration.* New York: David McKay, 1924.

Fox, Charles J. "Reinventing Government as Postmodern Symbolic

Politics." *Public Administration Review* 56 (1996): 256-262.

Foxall, Gordon, and Paul Hackett. "Consumer Satisfaction with Birmingham's International Convention Center." *Service Industries Journal* 14 (1994): 369-380.

Frederickson, George H. 1976. "The Lineage of New Public Administration." *Administration and Society* 8 (1976): 144-174.

Gabris Gerald T. "Monetary Incentives and Performance: Is There an Administratively Meaningful Connection?" In *Public Productivity Handbook*. Edited by Marc Holzer. New York: Marcel Dekker, 1992.

Gardner, Neely. "Power Diffusion in the Public Sector: Collaboration for Democracy." *Journal of Applied Behavioral Science* 10 (1974): 367-72.

Geier, J.G. "A Trait Approach to the Study of Leadership in Small Groups." *Journal of Communication* (December, 1991): 48-60.

Gigliotti, Linda. "An Adaption of Cameron's Model of Organizational Effectiveness at the Academic Department Level in Two-Year Community Colleges." Ph.D. diss., Syracuse University, 1988.

Goodnow, F.J., *Politics and Administration.* New York: The Macmillan Co.,1900.

Goodsell, Charles T. *The Case for Bureaucracy.* Chatham, N.J.: Chatham House Publishers, 1994.

Goodsell, Charles T. "The Grace Commission: Seeking Efficiency for the Whole People?" *Public Administration Review* (May/June, 1984): 196-205.

Gore, Al. *The Gore Report on Reinventing Government.* Washington: GPO, 1993

Gore, Al. *The Best Kept Secrets in Government.* Washington D.C.: GPO, 1996.

Gore, Al. *Common Sense Government: Works Better and Costs Less.* New York, New York: Random House, 1995.

Gouldner, Alvin. *Patterns of Industrial Bureaucracy.* New York: Free Press, 1954.

Griffin, R. "Consequences of Quality Circles in an Industrial Setting: A Longitudinal Assessment." *Academy of Management Journal* 21 (1988): 338-358.

Guy, Mary. (1992). "Managing People." In *Public Productivity Handbook.* Edited by Marc Holzer. New York: Marcel Dekker, 1992.

Gulick L. H. and L. Urwick, *Papers on the Science of Administration.* New York: Institute of Public Administration, 1937.

Hall, E.T., *The Silent Language*. New York: Doubleday, 1959.

Hambrick, D.C., and P.A. Mason. "Upper Echelons: The Organization as a Reflection of its Top Managers." *Academy of Management Review* (April,1984): 193-206.

Hammer, Michael. *Reengineering the Corporation*. New York: Harper Business, 1993.

Handfield, R. "Quality Management in Japan versus the United States: An Overview." *Production and Inventory Management* 30 (1989): 79-84.

Harrison, Roger. "Understanding Your Organization's Character." *Harvard Business Review* (May-June, 1972): 119-128.

Hart, David K., and David W. Hart. "Why the Gore Report will Probably Fail." *International Journal of Public Administration* 20 (1997): 183-220.

Herzberg, F., B. Mausner, and B. Synderman. *The Motivation to Work*. New York: Wiley, 1958.

Hibbert, Sally Ann. "The Marketing Positioning of British Medical Charities." *European Journal of Marketing* 29 (1995): 6-26.

Hoff, Joan. *Nixon Reconsidered*. New York: Basic Books, 1994.

Hofstede, G., B. Neuijen, D. Ohayv, and G. Sanders. "Measuring Organizational Cultures: A Qualitative and Quantitative Study Across Twenty Cases." *Administrative Science Quarterly* 35 (1990): 286-316.

Hoover Commission. *Report on Organization of the Executive Branch of Government*. New York: McGraw Hill, 1949.

Ingraham, Patricia W., and David H. Rosenbloom. "Political Foundations of the American Federal Service: Rebuilding A Crumbling Base." *Public Administration Review* 50 (1990): 210-219.

Ink, Dwight. "Does Reinventing Government Have an Achilles Heel." *Public Manager* 24(1996: 27-30.

Kachigan, Sam K. *Multivariate Statistical Analysis: A Conceptual Introduction*. New York: Radius, 1982.

Kanter-Moss, Rosabeth. *The Change Masters*. New York: Harper and Row, 1983

Kettl, D.F. *Reinventing Government: Appraising the National Performance Review*. Washington, DC: Brookings Institution, 1994.

King, Gary, Robert O. Keohane, and Sidney Verba. *Designing Social Inquiry: Scientific Inference in Qualitative Research*. Princeton, NJ: Princeton University Press, 1994.

Kirkpatrick, Shelley A., and Edwin A. Locke. "Leadership: Do Traits Matter." *Academy of Management Executive* (1991): 48-60.

Klein, J.A., "The Human Costs of Manufacturing Reform." *Harvard Business Review* 67 (1989): 60-66.

Kraines, Oscar. "The President Versus Congress: The Keep Commission, 1905-1909." *Western Political Quarterly* 23 (1970): 5-54.

Kreps, G.L. "Using Interpretative Research: The Development of a Socialization Program at RCA." In *Communication and Organizations* Edited by L.L. Putnam and M.E. Paconowsky Beverly Hills, CA: Sage Publications, Inc., 1983.

Lance, B. foreword to *Federal Reorganization: The Executive Branch.* by T.G. Fain. New York: Bowker, 1977.

Lawrence, B.S. "Historical Perspective: Using the Past To Study the Present." *Academy of Management Review.* 9 (1984): 307-312.

Likert, Rensis. *New Patterns of Management.* New York: McGraw Hill, 1961.

Lindbloom, Charles E. "The Science of Muddling Through." *Public Administration Review.* 19 (1959): 79-88.

Lipsky, Martin. *Street Level Bureaucracy.* New York: Russell Sage Foundation, 1980.

Louis, M.R. "Organizations as Culture Bearing Milieux." In *Monographs in Organizational Behavior and Industrial Relations.* Edited by L.R. Pondy, P.J. Frost, G. Morgan and T. C. Dandridge. Greenwich, CT: JAI Press, Inc., 1983

March, James G., and Johan P. Olsen. "Organizing Political Life: What Administrative Reorganization Tells Us About Government." *The American Political Science Review.* 77 (1983): 281-296.

March, James G., and Johan P. Olsen. *Rediscovering Institutions, The Organizational Basis of Politics.* New York: Free Press, 1989.

Marini, Frank. *Toward a New Public Administration: The Minnowbrook Perspective.* Scranton, PA: Chandler, 1972.

Martin, Joanne. *Cultures in Organizations: Three Perspectives.* New York: Oxford University Press, 1993.

Martz, Amy Elizabeth. "The Organizational Culture of the National Aeronautics and Space Administration: A Historical Analysis." Ph.D. diss., The Pennsylvania State University, 1990.

Maslow, A.H., and Murphy, G. *Motivation and Personality.* New York: Harper and Row, 1948.

McGregor, Douglas. "On Leadership." *Antioch Notes.* (May, 1954): 2-3.

McGregor, Douglas. *The Human Side of the Enterprise.* New York: McGraw-Hill, 1960.

Mead, M. *Coming of Age in Samoa.* New York: New American Library, 1949.

Meier, Kenneth J., *Politics and Bureaucracy.* North Scituate, MA: Duxbury Press, 1979.

Meyer, J., and B. Rowan. "Notes on the Structures of Educational Organizations." In *Studies on Environment and Organization.* Edited by B. Meyer. San Francisco: Jossey-Bass, 1977.

Meyer, A.D. "How Ideologies Supplant Formal Structures and Shape Environments." *Journal of Management Studies.* 28 (1982): 45-61

Meyer, Marshall. "Organizations and Sociology." In *Sociology in America.* Edited by Herbert Gans. Newbury Park, CA: Sage, 1990.

Miller, William H. "Reinventing Government: The Ultimate Management Challenge." *Industry Week.* 243 (1994): 65-68.

Mills, Michael. *Innovation and Change in Organizational Culture.* Ph.D. diss., University of Michigan, 1988.

Mintzberg, Henry. *The Nature of Managerial Work.* New York: Harper and Row, 1973.

Moe, Ronald C. "The Reinventing Government Exercise." *Public Administration Review.* 54 (1994): 111-122.

Mohr, Lawrence B. "Determinants of Innovation in Organizations." *American Political Science Review.* 63 (1969): 111-126.

Morgan, D.R., and J. P. Pelissero. "Urban Policy: Does Political Structure Matter?" *American Political Science Review.* 74 (1980): 999-1006.

Nathan, R.P. *The Plot That Failed: Nixon and the Administrative Presidency.* New York: Wiley, 1975.

National Commission on the Public Service. *Rebuilding the Public Service: The Report of the National Commission on the Public Service.* Washington, D.C.: GPO, 1989.

National Commission on the State and Local Public Service. *Hard Truths/Tough Choices: An Agenda for State and Local Reform.* Washington, D.C.: GPO, 1993.

Niehoff, B.P., C. A. Enz, and R. A. Grover. "The Impact of Top Management Actions on Employee Attitudes and Perceptions." *Group and Organization Studies.* (September, 1990): 337-352.

Nufrio, Philip M. "Diary of an Internal Consultant." *Group and Organization Studies.* (September,1983): 1-6.

Oakley, Ed and Doug Krug. *Enlightened Leadership: Getting to the Heart of Change.* New York: Simon and Schuster, 1993.

O'Reilly, C., J. Chatman, and D. Caldwell. "People and Organizational

Culture: A Q-Sort Approach to Easing Person-Organization Fit."
Academy of Management Journal. 34 (1991): 487-516.

Osborne, David and Theodore Gaebler. *Reinventing Government*.
Reading, MA: Addison-Wesley, 1992.

Osborne, D., and P. Plastrik. *Banishing Bureaucracy: The Five
Strategies for Reinventing Government*. New York: Addison-Wesley,
1997.

Ostrum, E., and V. Ostrum. "Public Choice: A Different Approach to
the Study of Public Administration." *Public Administration Review*.
31 (1971): 203-216.

Ouchi, William and A. Wilkins. "Organization Culture. "*Annual Review
of Sociology*. 11 (1985): 457-483.

Parsons, Talcott. *The Social System*. New York: Free Press, 1951.

Peters, Tom and Robert Waterman. In *Search of Excellence: Lessons
from America's Best Run Companies*. New York: Harper and Row,
1982.

Petrini, Frank. *The Rate of Adoption of Selected Agricultural
Innovations*. Upsupsala: Agricultural College of Sweden, 1966.

Pettigrew, Andrew. "On Studying Organization Culture." *Administrative
Science Quarterly*. 24 (1979): 570-581.

Pfeffer, Jeffrey. "Barriers to the Advance of
Organizational Science: Paradigm Development as a
DependentVariable." *Academy of Management Review*. 18(1992):
599-620.

President's Commission on Economy and Efficiency. *Report on the
Organization of the Government*. Washington, D.C: National
Archives, nd.

President's Committee on Administrative Management. *Administrative
Management in the Government of the United States*. Chicago, IL:
Public Administrative Service, 1937.

Presthus, Robert. *The Organizational Society*. New York: Martin's
Press, 1978.

Raju, Mohan P., and R.C Srivastava. "Factors Contributing to the
Teaching Profession." *International Journal of Education
Management*. 8(1984): 7-13.

Raturi, Anita. "Leadership and Organizational Culture in the Public
Sector: A Case Study of the Department of Energy." Ph.D. diss.,
University of Cincinnati, 1992.

Roethlisberger, F.J. and William J. Dickson. *Management and the
Worker*. Cambridge, MA: Harvard University Press, 1939.

Roethlisberger, F.J. and William J. Dickson. *Management and Morale.* Cambridge, MA: Harvard University Press, 1941.

Robertson, James Oliver. *American Myth, American Reality.* New York: Hill and Wang, 1980.

Rosenbloom, David H. "Democratic Constitutionalism and the Evolution of Bureaucratic Government: Freedom and Accountability in the Administrative State." In *The Constitution and American Political Development: An Institutional Perspective.* Edited by Peter F. Nardulli. University of Illinois Press, 1992.

Rourke, R.E. *Bureaucracy, Politics and Public Policy.* Boston: Little, Brown, 1969.

Rulnick, Adrienne. "Innovation and the Culture of Higher Education." Ph.D. diss., University of Massachusetts, 1991.

Sackman, Sonya A. "Uncovering Culture in Organizations." *Journal of Applied Behavioral Science.* (September, 1991): 295-317.

Sapienza, A.M. "Believing is Seeing: How Culture Influences the Decisions Top Managers Make," In *Gaining Control of the Corporate Culture* Edited by R.H. Kilman, M.J. Saxton and R. Serpa. San Francisco, CA: Jossey-Bass, 1985.

Sapienza, A.M. "Image Making as a Strategic Function: On the Language of Organizational Strategy." In *Organizations-- Communication.* Edited by L. Thayer. Norwood, NJ: Ablex Publishing, 1987.

Sapienza, A.M. "Imagery and Strategy," *Journal of Management.* 13 (1987): 343-555.

Sathe, V. "Implications of Corporate Culture: A Manager's Guide to Action." *Organizational Dynamics.* 12 (1983): 5-23.

Sathe, V. *Culture and Related Corporate Realities.* Homewood, IL: Richard D. Irwin, 1985.

Savas. E.S. *Privatizing the Public Sector: How to Shrink Government.* Chatham, New Jersey: Chatham House, 1982.

Savas, E.S. "Implementing Privatization." *Urban Resources.* 2(1985): 41.

Savas. E.S. *Privatization: The Key to Better Government.* Chatham, New Jersey: Chatham House, 1987.

Savas. E.S. Introduction to *Privatization for New York: Competing for a Better Future.* Laduer Commission. Albany: New York Senate Advisory Committee on Privatization, 1992.

Schachter, Hindy Lauer. "Reinventing Government or Reinventing Ourselves: Two Models for Improving Government Performance."

Public Administration Review. 55(1995): 530-537.

Schachter, Hindy Lauer. *Reinventing Government or Reinventing Ourselves: The Role of Citizen Owners in Making A Better Government.* Albany, New York: State University of New York Press, 1997.

Schein, Edgar. *Process Consultation.* Massachusetts: Addison-Wesley, 1976.

Schein, Edgar. "Coming to a New Awareness of Organizational Culture." *Sloan Management Review.* (Winter, 1984): 3-16.

Schein, Edgar. *Organization Culture and Leadership.* San Francisco: Jossey Bass, 1985.

Selznick, Philip. *TVA and the Grass Roots.* Berkeley: University of California Press, 1949.

Senge, Peter. *The Fifth Discipline: The Art and Practice of the Learning Organization.* New York: Doubleday, 1990.

Senge, Peter. *The Fifth Discipline Fieldbook.* New York: Doubleday, 1994.

Shepard, Herb A. "Changing Personal and Intergroup Relationships in Organizations." In *Handbook of Organizations* Edited by J. March Chicago: Rand-McNally, 1958.

Shoop, Tom. "The Reinvention Rage." *Government Executive.* 25 (1993): 10.

Shoop, Tom. "Exodus," *Government Executive.* 26 (1994): 42-47.

Siegel, Michael. "Reinventing Management in the Public Sector." *Federal Probation.* 60 (1996): 30.

Simon, Herbert A. "The Proverbs of Administration." *Public Administration Review.* 6 (1946): 53-67.

Simon, Herbert A. *Administrative Behavior: A Study of Decision Making Process in Administrative Organizations.* New York: Free Press, 1945, revised 1976.

Singh, Ram N. *Characteristic of Farm Innovations Associated with the Rate of Adoption.* Guelph: Ontario Agricultural Extension Education reprints, 1966.

Smelser, Neil J. *Theory of Collective Behavior.* New York: Free Press, 1962.

Spice, Martha. "Reinventing Government Leadership," *Public Manager.* 23(1994): 35-38.

Srivastva, Suresh and David L. Cooperrider. *Appreciative Management and Leadership.* San Francisco: Jossey Bass, 1990.

Steward, J.H. *Theory of Cultural Change.* Urbana: University of

Changing Organizational Culture: A Study of the National Government 131

Illinois Press, 1955.

Stratton, Brad. "Four More Years of Reinventing Government," *Quality Progress*. 30 (1997): 45-46.

Tannenbaum, Robert. "Training Managers for Leadership." *Personnel*. 30 (1954): 3-6.

Taylor, Frederick W. *Shop Management*. Harper and Row, New York, 1903.

Taylor, Frederick W. *The Principles of Scientific Management*. New York: Harper, 1911.

Taylor, Frederick W. *Scientific Management*. Harper and Row, New York, 1923.

Terry, Larry D. *Leadership of Public Bureaucracies*. London: Sage Publications, 1995.

Thomas, James B., Laura J. Shankster, and John E. Mathieu. "Antecedents to Organization Issues Interpretation: The Roles of Single-Level, Cross-Level, and Content Cues." *Academy of Management Journal*. 37(1994): 1252-1284.

Thompson, Frank J. *Revitalizing State and Local Public Service*. San Francisco: Jossey-Bass, 1993.

Thompson, Frank J., and Vernon D. Jones. "Reinventing the Federal Government: The Role of Theory in Reform Implementation." *American Review of Public Administration*. 25 (1995): 183-199.

Thompson, Frank J. "The Reinvention Revolution." *Government Executive*. 28(1996): 39-41.

Topolosky, Betty. *Culture and Innovation in Higher Education: A Semiotic Study*. Ph.D. diss., Ohio University, 1989.

Torbert, William R. Review of *Reasoning, Learning and Action* by Chirs Argyris. *Harvard Educational Review*. (1982): 226-229.

Trice, H.M. and Beyer, J.M. "Cultural Leadership in Organizations." *Organization Science*. (May, 1991): 149-169.

Triste, Eric L. "Working with Bion in the 1940's: The Group Decade." In *Bion and Group Psychotherapy*. Edited by M. Pines. London: Routledge and Kegan Paul, 1985.

Van Maanen, J. "Reclaiming Qualititative Methods for Organizational Research: A Preface." *Administrative Science Quarterly*. 24 (1979): 520-526.

Van Maanen, John. *Tales of the Field: On Writing Ethnography*. Chicago: University of Chicago Press, 1988.

Van Riper, P.P. "The Politics-Administration Dichotomy: Concept or Reality?" In *Politics and Administration: Woodrow Wilson and*

American Public Administration. Edited by J. Rabin and J.S. Bowman. New York: Marcel Dekker, 1984.

Weber, Max. *Economy and Society: An Outline of Interpretative Sociology.* Translated by Guenther Roth and Claus Wittich. New York: Bedminister Press, 1968.

Weick, K. "Educational Organizations as Loosely Coupled Systems." *Administrative Science Quarterly.* 21 (1976): 1-19.

Weisboard, Marvin. *Productive Workplaces: Organizing and Managing for Dignity, Meaning and Community.* San Francisco: Jossey-Bass, 1990.

Weisenbeck, Marlene. *Organizational Culture and Faculty Motivation: Faculty and Administrative Perspectives.* Ph.D. diss., The University of Wisconsin, 1989.

White, L.D. "Administration, Public." In *Encyclopedia of the Social Sciences.* New York: The Macmillan Co., 1933.

Willoughby, W.F. *Principles of Public Administration.* Washington, D.C. The Brookings Institution, 1927.

Wilson, Woodrow. "The Study of Administration." *Political Science Quarterly.* 2 (1887): 197-222.

Winograd, G.R. "A Holonomic Interpretative Model for an Organizational Culture: Multiple Dimensions of Holotexts." Paper presented at the Annual meeting of Eastern Communication Association, Syracuse, New York, 1987.

York, Byron. "Al's Big Scam," *American Spectator.* 29 (1996): 38.

INDEX